CHANGES:
From Spiritual Hopelessness to Spiritual Hope

**One Woman's
Search for God:**
The Discovery

Carlotta Maria Shinn Russell

Copyright © 2022 by Carlotta Maria Shinn Russell.

ISBN 978-1-64133-864-6 (softcover)
ISBN 978-1-64133-863-9 (ebook)

All rights reserved. No part of this book may be reproduced or transmitted in any form or by any means, electronic or mechanical, including photocopying, recording, or by any information storage and retrieval system without express written permission from the author, except in the case of brief quotations embodied in critical reviews and certain other noncommercial uses permitted by copyright law.

Printed in the United States of America.

Brilliant Books Literary
137 Forest Park Lane Thomasville
North Carolina 27360 USA

This book is dedicated to my husband who supported me in every change I have gone through. He has loved me and learned to understand and accept me for who I am. He stood behind me even when he didn't agree with the method or the idea. All of my love and admiration goes to my husband, Timothy Bert Russell, Sr., for his love and support.

For what is a man profited, if he shall gain the whole world, and lose his own soul? Or what shall a man give in exchange for his soul.

—*Matthew 16:26; Mark 8:37*

Contents

"A Psalm of Life" by Henry Wadsworth Longfellow vii

Author's Page ix

Introduction xi

Chapter 1: The Gift 1
Chapter 2: The Hurricane Rushes In 19
Chapter 3: The Gentle Breeze 23
Chapter 4: The Fading Rose 29
Chapter 5: The Dilemma 31
Chapter 6: The Grizzly 35
Chapter 7: The Pain in Loving 37
Chapter 8: The Long Way Home 41
Chapter 9: Straddling the Fence 45
Chapter 10: The Journey Begins 49
Chapter 11: The Mountain 59
Chapter 12: Joy Comes in the Morning 61
Chapter 13 65
The Clouds Are Gone 65
Chapter 14 75
The Finished Life 75

Chapter 15: Life's Lessons: A Mother's Wisdom 81
Chapter 16: Conclusion: The New Man 85

References 95

About the Author 97

About the Book 99

A Psalm of Life

Life is real! Life is earnest!
And the grave is not its goal;
Dust thou are, to dust thou returnest,
Was not spoken of the soul,

—Henry Wadsworth Longfellow

Author's Page

Sage Mariah Seymour graciously agreed to talk with me about herself as a young adult between the age of twenty-one and thirty years of age; her family life; and how tragedy, pain, suffering, and the loss of her sister and her mother to an evil disease within seven months of each other took an amazing toll on her and her family, but especially her. Sage's faith was shaken to the core as a result of these losses, especially since she had carried the same disease in her body during a crucial time in her life. The losses damaged her relationship with God and her family and she chose to be friends with the world. This journey took her away from God, and the same journey brought her back to God. The journey she took, further tried the very fabric of her being, and tested her faith beyond endurance. This was at a very trying and dark time in her life. Karl, her husband, at that time from1972 through 1979, was not supportive, nor did he seem to grasp the severity of the situation. She felt as if she was alone with all the losses she suffered with nowhere to turn, but to the world.

Sage Mariah Seymour, I found, was very pleasant. She is a very spiritual person who has very strong beliefs in God. She is a follower of Jesus Christ, her Lord and Savior. Sage is a very self-effacing individual. Modesty was very evident to me in this very strong and fragile natured individual. There was almost, an aloofness about her to the point of her seeming to be a very a secluded, a very private person, until I got to know her better. She is joyful person, who loves to laugh, with an amazing reflective mind.

It was very heart wrenching to hear her reveal a very private and heartbreaking time in her life. I appreciated the time she took to share with me the following account of this tragedy. When I asked her why she agreed to tell me of a very private matter that is so close to her heart, she said, "There many women and men, who go through heartbreaking times in their life and do not know where to turn or who to turn to. They feel they have no hope. But, she wanted them to know about my experience and how I survived and dealt with the tragedy, heartaches and hard lesson learned. there is hope, but that hope lies in one person only."

One of Sage's sons said to me about his mother that she was a, "Confident, inspiring, accomplished, strong, and amazing—a very special mother; a wonderful woman who he and his brother is very proud of." These qualities are not rare in a mother, but it is hard to find children that will talk to you about their mother in this manner.

Sage is a very accomplished individual. She is talented and has a very versatile set of skills. Sage is a Seamstress, she makes her own clothes, as well as creates her own patterns and styles; she is a writer; she is a University Professor; she teaches Ladies Bible Class at her church; as well as, writes her own lesson and she is very knowledgeable of Scripture.

I found that she is an exciting person to know, as well as, to be around. Sage talked to me over a period of a year from 2009-2010. She is warm, engaging, full of vitality, energetic, strong, amazing, and is all ways ready for a new challenge. I could readily see why her son was so proud to call her his mother. Rarely, have I met a person like Sage Mariah Seymour-even her name is not typical, not for that that day and time and that part of the country. There are many women in the world that suffer in silence. She urges women everywhere to share their story with someone; it is therapeutic and could possibly give someone hope.

I wrote the book based on the facts that she dictated to me of her young life. Sage is now in her late 50's and is a very strong and spiritual. She is grounded in her faith with her feet planted firmly on a road and on a journey that will take her to eternal life and peace at last with the tragedies she suffered.

Sage is from Chunchula, Alabama where she grew up and lived most of her life there. She now lives in the city limits of Mobile, Alabama.

Introduction

This book is devoted to all women (and men) who have gone through many trials and tribulations in their lives, who have come full-circle, and who have had to face life and situations as is—women who can put aside their play putty and know they cannot shape the world and control the situations around them. Women sometimes look at the world through *rose-colored* glasses, rather than realistically. Life is hard to fact, therefore skewing the facts makes it easier to deal with life's troubles; hiding is at times more attractive than facing the reality of a situation. We as women must force ourselves to accept situations "as is" and have the strength and willingness to change with the situations and problems and accept and deal with heartaches that come into our lives. These situations and problems are like strong gusts of wind. Women often create a situation in their mind that makes dealing with life's tragedies easier-they will skew the facts to make their life less painful.

Life is not a constant "beating" upon you; Women need a shelter from these strong gusts of wind in those unbearable times. God is that shelter; He is a providential God. He is ever with us through all our trials and tribulations. Sometimes we must go on the journey called *change* to open our eyes so we can see the shelter. We walk past it often, at least once a day. God is a strong mountain that does not move. His shelter comes only if we take the journey back to the mountain.

Changes in life are like the shifting sands of the Sahara. Like the sands, life is unpredictable. There are always underlying factors that cause these sudden shifts. We as humans are so unaccustomed to sudden shifts in our lives that we sometimes indulge in the luxury of complacency. Complacency is a lonely island, a mirage that fades the closer we get to reality. Complacency can bury us like the desert sands. Changes in our lives can build walls that are not easy to get over.

Life is an unconquerable part of humanity. Life and its events can be fierce and changing. The trials that beset humans are inhospitable and unforgiving. Hope becomes elusive. Humans sometimes chase hope like the pot of gold at the end of the rainbow. There within life's shifting sands lies hopelessness.

Humans as a whole think they can direct their steps and set their own courses in life. This is a false lure that draws man in. It is akin to a rock falling off a mountain; it continues to tumble without hope. Man's attempt to design his own path and his own steps for life is like waging an unwinnable war with life and its vicious, unforgiving nature. Changes have an enchanting sound until this unwinnable war ensues. Man's devising ways of setting his own path to God is a fleeting effort. Man can change, but God does not. The Scripture tells us that God said, "I am The Lord Thy God, and I change not" (Mal. 3:6, King James Version).

Man has a shifting-sands attitude, thinking he can go in any direction without the assistance of the Father in heaven. With this attitude, we are in a state of hopelessness. Hopelessness can be defined as man without God. Before we can correct this attitude, we must first realize that we are in this state. Denying that we need God's assistance is as dangerous to our spiritual salvation as overdosing on pills. Overdosing puts us in a state of unawareness, as does the attitude of living and planning our lives without God's assistance.

Separating ourselves from the shadow of the Almighty leaves us hopeless. God cannot work in our lives if we do not allow Him. Matthew 23:37 tells that Jesus said, "I would have gathered you under my wings as a mother hen does her chicks, but you would not." But you would not. Man has to let God lead his life, and he has to depend on Him, knowing that He is the maker and giver of all life and that He does not make mistakes.

Humans make the mistake of thinking they can direct their paths and plan their every step, thereby living without God. Anger toward God is another falling rock; there is no benefit in anger toward God.

Therefore, let's not live in a state of spiritual hopelessness but in a state of spiritual hope, looking to Jesus, the author and finisher of our faith (Heb. 12:2).

In addition, photographs are good depictions of reality; they show every aspect of the item or person photographed. Even though a photo may show perfection, life is not perfect; however, there can be perfect moments in our lives. Humans sometimes live as silhouettes, with no depth or permanency to themselves. Silhouettes are just shadows of a life. Can you really see what a silhouette is? You can change it to look any way you want. In contrast to a photo, a silhouette has no permanency.

As such, life is like a puzzle you put together once piece at a time. Oftentimes puzzles have a picture or some scenery of life on them. As the pieces are put together, it can depict life. We like some pieces of the puzzle more than others, just you like some parts and pieces of your life more than others.

Sage Seymour pictured her life like a puzzle; there were parts of her life she liked and other parts of her life she did not.

Malachi 3:6: I am the Lord; I change not.

Matthew 23:37: O Jerusalem, Jerusalem, thou that killeth the prophets, and stonest them which are sent unto thee, how often would I have gathered thy children together, even as a hen gathereth her chickens under her wings, and ye would not.

Hebrews 12:2: Looking to Jesus the Author and Finisher or Our Faith; who for the joy that was set before him endured the cross, despising the shame, and is set down at the right hand of the throne of God.

Sage's childhood was the part of the picture on the puzzle she loved. But in contrast, her adult life she did not like, especially the years between the ages of twenty-one and thirty. The Seymour family suffered too many loses. During those years, Sage saw heartbreak, pain, and agony inflicted by an evil disease that destroyed minds and spirits and drained the very souls of the Seymour family members.

Sage's life was filled with dark valleys and shadowy places for many years. The gift of light eluded her and her family. Trying to find some light and solace in the world seemed like trying to catch the wind rustling through the beautiful oak trees that stood so silently and tall in Chunchula as if they were watching the Seymour family's life happen. Events unfolded, it seemed, on a continual basis; there was no peace or rest for the family for many years.

The events took a devastating toll on the family, especially Sage, her sister Dysantha, and her mother, Maria. Evil lurks in the world. It is ever-present with everyone, every day. Satan is the author and ochestrator of all evil in the world (John 8:44; 2 Cor. 11:3). He does not intend to spend eternity by himself, but rather he wants to take as many souls as possible to his eternity of damnation.

Whether you feel life is a glass that is half full or half empty, describing life that way brings man to the same place: life has no meaning, no value, no future without God, for His Word is the truth and the life (John 1:4). Without God, there is only a physical or worldly life (Gen. 2:17).

John 8:44: Ye are of your father the devil, and the lusts of your father will ye do. He was a murder from the beginning, and abode not in the truth, because there is no truth in him. When he speaketh a lie, he speaketh on his own: for he is a liar, and the father of it.

2 Corinthians 11:3: But I am afraid that just as Eve was deceived by the serpent's cunning, your minds may somehow be led astray from your sincere and pure devotion to Christ.

John 1:4: In him was life, and the life was the light of men.

Genesis 2:17: But the tree of the knowledge of good and evil you shall not eat, for in the day that you eat of it ye shall surely die.

Changes: The Beginning

Changes in life are inevitable. Each situation brings about a change as well as dictates it. Changes in life can be good or bad, but good changes that produce positive characteristics in humans are a plus. In contrast, changes that are bad can also be good and produce positive characteristics in human beings. The Preacher, Jesus, tells us in Psalms 30:5, "Crying [weeping] may endure for a night, but joy comes in the morning." Nights linger long as we wait for our mornings to come. Changes bring about many joyful mornings in our lives. However, changes—whether good or bad—come with a high price.

Genesis 2:19 tells us, "Out of the ground God formed every beast of the field and every fowl of the air and bought them to Adam to name." Eve was born into this wealth. Man calls it being born with a silver spoon in one's mouth. Everything needed for life was already there when God made Eve. She lacked nothing upon her day of arrival. And with the rib the Lord God had taken from man, he made a woman and brought her unto man (Gen. 2:22). Every day, Eve had the privilege to walk and talk with God in the Garden of Eden in the cool of the evening. And she and Adam heard the voice of God walking in the garden in the cool of the day (Gen. 3:8). Her daily contact and spiritual meals with God brought about a positive change; she was happy, joyful and at peace.

When a child is fed nourishing food, he or she grows to be a healthy individual. Eve fed on the Word of God on a one-on-one basis every day. She loved God and His Creation. Galatians 5:22–27 gives a vivid picture of the fruit of the spirit. Eve possessed this fruit while she walked with God each day. This is fruit in a collective sense. In comparison with Eve, we as women can also possess the fruit of the spirit. When it comes to spiritual fruit, there are different levels and different kinds such as: love, joy, peace, and longsuffering. We don't always have the strength and wisdom to know what God would have us to do or how to please him in our daily walk with him. We as humans all have weaknesses. We might be stronger in some of the fruit of the spirit than in others. Or we can possess all levels as Eve did.

Sage was not sure that she possessed all the fruit of the spirit. Bearing this type of fruit was a difficult change for her. She had never seen herself as the spiritual being the Bible described as a fruitful person. Neither did she possess what the Bible said a fruitful person possesses. Becoming this type of spiritual person would be a big change for her. Could she possess he same relationship with God that Eve had?

> *Galatians 5:22–27: But the fruit of the spirit is love, joy, peace, longsuffering, gentleness, goodness, faith, meekness, temperance: against such there is no law. And they that are Christ's have crucified the flesh with the affections and lusts. If we live in the spirit, let us also walk in the spirit. Let us not be desirous of vain glory, provoking one another, envying one another.*

For a brief while, Eve enjoyed a relationship with God that few women could ever imagine. She spoke and interacted with eternity on a daily basis. The knowledge and wisdom she had the opportunity to obtain and possess is one of which no university can boast.

Theodore Roosevelt said, "A thorough knowledge of the Bible is worth more than a college education," (The Bible Reader's Journal, 2001). Sage said she would rephrase this statement to say, "A thorough knowledge of *God* is worth more than a college education." Many people know what the Bible says, but that is not the same as knowing God. The Bible tells us we get to know God through personal relationships with him. A dialogue must be created. Buber said, "God can only be known by means of personal relationships with God. Dialogue embodies a special kind of communication," (1923, 216).

Eve had the chance to have a thorough knowledge of God. The Tree of Knowledge was a plant in the middle of the Garden of Eden used to prove the first couple's loyalty to the Creator (Gen. 2:3). But the serpent tempted Eve to eat it and to become like God, knowing good and evil (Gen. 3:5). Eating the forbidden fruit or listening to the voice of Satan (or the world) resulted in shame, guilt, exclusion from the Garden, and separation from the Tree of Knowledge and God (*The Master Bible, King James Version, Tree of Knowledge* 2001, B-490).

The Tree of Knowledge symbolized access to eternal life, and Eve's relationship with God changed radically when she and Adam sinned.

That symbol of wisdom (Proverbs 3:18) is within human limits, but she chose to listen to the voice of a stranger, a stranger she had not met before:

> Now, the serpent was more crafty then any of the animals that the Lord God had made. He said to the woman, "Has God not said, 'You shall not eat from the trees of the garden'?" The woman said to the serpent, "We may eat fruit from the tress in the garden, but God said, 'You must not eat fruit from the tree that is in the middle of the garden, and you must touch it, or you will die. "You will not surely die," the serpent said to the woman. For God knows that when you eat of it, your eyes will be opened, and you will be like God, knowing good and evil." When the woman saw that the fruit of the tree was good for food and pleasing to the eye, and also desirable for gaining wisdom, she took some and ate it (Genesis 3:1–6).

She had talked with God and interacted with eternity more than once. But this choice brought about a change in her life that would deprive her of her daily interaction with the God of eternity. It was an event that changed the entire course of the world and human nature. Eve's life had been positive up to that point, but all too soon that relationship changed radically, and the rebuilding (man making his way back to God) started.

Sage chose to listen to the voice of a stranger just as Eve did, and her choice—like Eve's—was the tail of a hurricane (the part of the storm that is even more devastating than the front). Both women's actions were sins.

The trials Sage would go through would test her beyond her strength. She would be torn between the world she had always known (the one she had created for herself) and the spiritual world the Scripture commands humans must be a part of (meaning we cannot make our own worlds).

Sage thought of creating her own world in terms of clay putty children use to play games or create images. It would be a kinder world if each of us could use clay putty to create an image of the world in which we want to live. The type of changes the Scripture requires was beyond what Sage was able or willing to give. Like man, Sage thought God presented her with a hard prescription for life. Sage was twenty-one years of age at this time.

At this point in Sage's life, she did not know of what fabric her emotional or spiritual self was made. At this point, questions and doubts loomed over her life like a heavy cloud before a hurricane rushes in.

With all the changes that take place, life has a way of getting off course. We go through phases of identity and getting to know ourselves. Sometimes we really don't know who we are until a tragedy or some other devastation besets our lives.

Maturity does not mean we are old, but rather it is an indication how much life we've seen and the experiences that have brought us to this point. Maturity comes not with age but with understanding, as the Preacher tells us in Proverbs 3:13. Then again, do we know where we are? We wrestle with these types of questions for long periods of time until we can understand. Sometimes it takes taking a journey back to our childhoods to discover the answer to "who" we are. The answer can be buried in our childhoods because time buries our childhoods in our memories.

> *Proverbs 3:13: Blessed is the one who finds wisdom, and the one who gets understanding.*

Inhabitants of Spiritual Eden

Sage knew in her mind and spirit that she and any other woman of God could enjoy the same privilege Eve had with God: to walk in the Garden in the cool of the day. Each woman of God possesses or can possess her own Garden of Eden—that is, a spiritual garden. We can all possess or inhabit that garden. God has granted us the ability to walk with Him there. We can be spiritually fed just as Eve was on a daily basis through the Scripture, the Word of God.

But a major change had taken place in the life of Sage Alyantha Seymour-Jacobson. She no longer looked at the walk with God as a literal walk but rather as a spiritual walk. This change came in Sage's life in 1975 before there was no hint of tragedy on the horizon. But to come to this level of Christianity, she had to stop looking through the lens of the camera of life with a mortal eye and look through the lens with a spiritual eye and the lens cap caps off. Change sometimes brings "shaded" areas with it. Her lack of complete understanding left shaded areas. Sage did not completely understand the entire concept of God or Christianity.

As Eve was fed daily with spiritual meals on her walks with God, so can the Christian woman of any century be fed. Our spiritual Gardens of Eden and our meetings with God can be on the swing, in the rose garden, in the car as we drive down the road, or it can be in all of these places. We meet God on a daily basis in the spirit. Though it would be wonderful to meet Him literally and see Him face-to-face as Eve did.

Sage said, "We must remember God is flexible. He is not obsessed with clock time as man is. He has an expectation time for humans; He expects us to keep His word, perform our Christian duty, and avoid distractions."

Because the days are evil, we must redeem the time by walking circumspectfully (Eph. 5:15–17); we must stay watchful, not letting our guard down as Eve did. For just one moment she let her desires about life and the unknown and what the future might hold take over. That one moment of letting her guard down had a long-reaching effect. Look to God, be fed on His given Word, and not try to write your own prescription for life.

> *Ephesians 5:15-17: See that you walk circumspectfully, not as fools, but as wise, redeeming the time, because the days are evil. Wherefore be ye not unwise, but understanding what the will of the Lord is.*

We are not spiritual or physical doctors; we are not qualified to write prescriptions in life or for life. God wrote the prescription of pattern for life for us as He did for Eve. He told Moses when to make the tabernacle: "for, See, said he, that you make all things according to the pattern shewed to thee in the mount" (Hebrews 8:5). He has not changed His prescription or patterns for mankind; it is still His Word. His Word is life. His Word is a lamp unto my feet and a light unto my pathway, (Ps. 119:105). Eve stepped outside of that light for a moment. We can so easily do the same if we are not walking circumspectfully. We are not to walk in our own way (Acts 14:16). God's Son is the sum of the Scripture. He fulfilled the requirements and set the example. He resisted every way Satan tried to tempt him. He walked circumpectfully.

We can try the patience of God by walking in a way contrary to the Scripture. Humans have the attitude of "sometimeness," but God is not a "sometimey" God. He does not straddle a spiritual fence as we do. We play the hypocrite, trying to live in both worlds as Eve did; our sins, like her sins did, will all too soon find us out. We play a childish game of hide-and-seek with God when we sin; He know all things and where we are at all times, both spiritually and physically. Therefore, as inhabitants of our spiritual Gardens of Eden, we must not allow worldly distractions and desires to cause us to be evicted from our spiritual homes as Eve was evicted from her physical home. We have everything we need for life and salvation through the Scripture and our daily spiritual walks with God. We must feed on the fat, the wine, marrow, and the lees of the Word of God (Isa. 25:6). This is a healthy diet, a spiritual diet.

Life itself is a serpent in a tree with sweet luring words and wonderful promises. But life will let you down and deprive you of living and enjoying that spiritual walk with God in the spiritual Eden. These daily meals can bring into our lives—as they did in Eve's life—peace, joy, happiness, and a deep, abiding love for God and His creation.

Sage had thought she possessed all of these fruits and had that walk in her spiritual Eden with God until the trials of life tried the very fabric of her soul and tragedy struck.

The road to the spiritual Garden of Eden bears to the right. We cannot be in spiritual error and please God. God reprimands the inhabitants of His spiritual Eden as He did Eve in His physical Eden. Though Eve may not have lost eternity, a change took place in her life. She had to learn obedience through the things she suffered, just as we must learn obedience in our spiritual Edens through the things we suffer (Heb. 5:8).

> *Acts 14:16: Who in times past suffered all nations to walk in their own ways.*
>
> *Hebrews 8:5: For, See, said he, that you make all things according to the pattern shewed to thee in the mount.*
>
> *Hebrews 5:8: Although Jesus was a son; he learned obedience by the things which he suffered.*
>
> *Psalms 119:105: His word is a lamp unto my fee and a light for my pathway.*
>
> *Isaiah 25:6: And in this mountain shall the Lord of host make unto all people a feast of fat things, a feast of wines on the lees, of fat things full of marrow, of wines on the lees well refined.*

Sage, age 50 now, said, "In her reflection, had to learn obedience, God is in control and His word stands; for He is the Master of the Universe." And Sage finally realized that she was part of the universe. All of this knowledge came with her journey down the road called "the world." All too soon Sage, like the Prodigal Son, found out that home is in the safety of the Father, and it is the only place we can find peace and joy and live lives that are pleasing to God. But before this knowledge came the heartbreaking journey for Sage.

The journey of Sage Alyantha Seymour begins as the story unfolds…

Chapter 1

The Gift

Sage was still very young in 1976 when she had her second child, a boy she named Chester Michael Jacobson. She saw her second son as a "gift" from God. Even though all children are gifts from God, Chester was different; he was not supposed to be here. His mother, Sage, had the alternative of having an abortion or carrying her baby to full term in the face of risk and deadly disease.

At that time, Sage had been married to her husband, Karl Jacobson, for six years. Four years and five months earlier, she'd had her first son, Charles Matthew Jacobson. Charles was a very sweet child, with long, curly hair, black eyes set behind very long eyelashes, and an endearing smile that warmed the heart.

Sage was not the strongest person [at that time]; she had been fragile health-wise all her life. However, Charles had been born by C-section, and he was a perfectly beautiful child. But Chester had lots of odds that could have prevented his birth. It was not that Sage did not want Chester, but because of the years that passed without her becoming pregnant again, she had assumed she would have one child. But time proved her wrong.

Sage learned she was pregnant for the second time in the most unusual way. One day, she got dizzy while standing in the bathroom in the master bedroom. The room spun around her like a whirlwind. She could not see, and she could not control the dizziness, so she ended up on the floor while the room continued to swirl. Sage called her son, Charles, and had him to run down the fencerow to get her mother, Maria.

Sage lived in the country. There were no street names, not even a lane. Her comment to Charles was, "Run down the fencerow and get Granny."

Charles did as asked, a brave little four-and-a-half-year-old boy. Sage would have been worried if she had lived in the city limits. It would have been far too dangerous for a four-year-old to try to get help; crossing the street would have been out of the question.

Maria arrived after about ten minutes and got Sage into bed. The dizziness finally subsided after her mother applied cold compresses to her head and around her neck.

"What happened, dear?" Maria asked.

"I was washing my hands and turned to get a towel to dry them," Sage said. "I don't remember anything else until I was on the floor and the room was spinning."

> *Psalms 127:3 says that, "Lo Children are a heritage of the Lord; and the fruit of the womb is his reward.*

Sage felt very nauseated. Her mom just stood and smiled after she described the symptoms.

"Sage, you are pregnant," Maria said.

"No, Mother, you are mistaken," Sage replied. "It has to be something else."

"I am almost as sure you are pregnant as I am that you are my baby daughter," Maria said.

Sage refused to accept this as fact. It had not sunken in yet. She had thought she would have only one child because her physicians had told her one C-section was all any one woman could have. She was frightened and upset by the possibility of having a second child; but the next day,

March 12, 1976, the doctor confirmed for Sage, a week later what her mother had told her.

The gynecologist examined Sage with the usual procedure; he took a Pap smear to test and confirm pregnancy. During the exam and test, the gynecologist told Sage that he was sending her sample to a lab for confirmation of the pregnancy, which usually took seven days to the test.

> *Psalms 127:3 says that, "Lo Children are a heritage of the Lord; and the fruit of the womb is his reward.*

March 12 would prove to be a very gloomy day for Sage. After arriving with her mother at the doctor's office, she was taken right in to see Doctor Tonsmeyer and Doctor Braun without delay, which seemed strange to Sage; she usually had to wait to see the doctor. Doctor Tonsmeyer would be the attending physician for her pregnancy with Dr. Braun as the consulting physician. His specialty was surgery. He would be the attending surgeon. If she was pregnant, she was not far enough along to be given the preference her doctor's office gave their mothers-to-be.

Sage's doctor asked her and her mother to be seated. Naturally, the doctor exchanged pleasantries with her as usual. Being warm and casual and having a good bedside manner are some of the many wonderful attributes of any Southerner, especially a doctor.

"What were the results of the … ah … test?" Sage asked the doctor.

"Sage, I have good news for you; you are about six weeks pregnant," the doctor said.

Thinking back, Sage remembered getting thick around her middle, but she had attributed it to eating well. She had never even dawned on her that she was pregnant.

"Doctor, I thought it was dangerous for me to have another child by C-section," she commented.

She had found out with the birth of her first child that her hips were built to narrowly to birth a child naturally. When her water broke with her first child, she had only dilated about one-fourth of a centimeter. Sage had also found out then that she was a free bleeder; she had a hemophiliac blood condition. A week before her delivery, she had been sent home with blood coagulators to thicken her blood for the C-section surgery.

"Yes, that is true, but you are healthy, so it should be no problem," Dr. Tonsmeyer said. "We will take the baby at thirty-seven weeks and not allow you to get to forty-two weeks as you did with your first child. We did not know at that time that you could not birth a child naturally, nor did we know you had the blood condition."

Dr. Tonsmeyer and Dr. Braun told Sage that they would monitor her progress on a weekly basis throughout the pregnancy.

Sage, nervous and scared, turned to her mother and asked her in a most despairing tone, "Mama, what should I do? I am not sure I can do this."

As usual, Maria smiled. She softly took Sage's hand in hers and gripped it firmly. "Sage look at me; I know you are frightened, even scared, and you have a right to be concerned, but think first of the child you are carrying. It is another life, possibility a little Sage. You said you wanted a girl."

"Yes, it is true, Mama," Sage said. "But I want the baby to have a mother to raise it. According to what Dr. Tonsymeyer and Dr. Braun are saying, they could lose me during the surgery."

"Sage," Maria said to her daughter, "You seem to have forgotten that you have a Father in heaven who loves you, and your faith and trust in Him will help get you through this pregnancy."

Sage thought for a while and said, "I do have faith in God, and I will trust that He will help me get through this pregnancy." I know that Matthew 7:7: "Ask and it shall be given, seek and you shall find and knock and it shall be opened unto you". Also, Hebrew 11:1: "Now faith is the substance of thing hoped for, the evidence of things not seen." There is nothing man cannot do with faith in God, as long as it is as God so wills. But when we ask, we cannot waver as the waves that are tossed or have doubt that God can perform it, as explained in James 1:6.

"There is more news, Sage, and it is not good," Dr. Tonsmeyer said.

Sage wondered what be worse than the prospect of her unborn child not surviving. Dr. Tonsmeyer told Sage that her Pap smear had come back a "three."

"A three?" Sage said. "What does this mean?" At this time in her life, Sage was not familiar with the levels of tests in relation to Pap smears.

"This test indicates that there is a problem with your uterus, your ovaries, or some other area of your lower extremities," Dr. Tonsmeyer said. "It could also be that you have a female infection due to too much yeast in your body. It is doubtful that it is an infection, but we need to know." He told Sage he wanted her to go the Providence Hospital to have a test taken; they would take a biopsy of her uterus.

"What does all of this mean?" Sage asked Dr. Tonsmeyer.

He told her that he did not want to venture an opinion or give a diagnosis without having the facts. He then told her when to report for her biopsy and that it would take seven to ten days to get the results.

Seven more days? Sage thought. She asked the doctor how this affected the baby she was carrying.

"Sage, I can't tell you that either until I know the results of the tests," he replied.

After the test, Sage left Providence Hospital with lots of questions in her mind. She waited anxiously and prayerfully until finally, after ten days, Dr. Tonsmeyer and Dr. Braun's office called for her to come for the results of her test. With her mother at her side, she went reluctantly. On the trip down, Sage asked her mother if she had told her father, Jacque, about the test.

Maria's response to her daughter was, "Yes, I have. He was overjoyed about the baby. But when he learned about the possibility that there was something else wrong, he did not say anything. He has sat, when he's at home, just swinging his leg, with his head hung down and his eyes closed."

"I have been so consumed with playing the game of 'what if' and wondering what the eventuality of what the future might be, I did not think to talk with him about it," Sage said.

"He understands you better than you think," Maria told her daughter. "We have both prayed every minute that God will be with you whatever the situation is and for Him to help you make the right decision. Sage, you might have to make some hard decisions before the day is through. I want you to be strong and lean on your faith in God and the belief that He will get you through this."

"I have faith and believe that God is in control of the situation," Sage told her mother.

After arriving at the doctor's office, Sage was immediately taken in to see Dr. Tonsmeyer and Dr. Braun. Dr. Tonsmeyer came around the desk to sit in front of Sage and her mother.

He took Sage's hand and said, "Sage, I don't want to prolong this any further. Neither do I want to minimize the seriousness of the situation, but you have to make some hard choices to make over the next few weeks."

"Dr. Tonsmeyer, what are the results of the test?" Sage asked.

"Sage, you have malignant cancer on the mouth of your uterus," Dr. Tonsmeyer said.

"Doctor, how can this be? I am pregnant," she said.

"It can be, and it is," he replied.

"What am I to do? I cannot carry a child and have this evil disease growing on my uterus. The child I carry is inside my uterus, is it not?" she said.

"Yes. It is a very difficult situation, I know, but you do have some choices," Dr. Tonsmeyer said.

"What are they, the choices, I mean? Dr. Tonsmeyer, I have both life and death growing inside of me at the same time. I don't understand how this can be. How can I get pregnant with cancer growing on my uterus?"

"I don't know, Sage," Dr. Tonsmeyer said. "I don't have a medical answer for you that will make any sense to you at this time."

By this point in the conversation, Dr. Tonsmeyer had moved into the chair to Sage's left, where he continued to hold her hand. Maria was seated on the right, holding her daughter's right hand with the same firm fervency she always had when there was trouble in the family. Sage had a momentary flashback of her childhood, with her mother always by her side in any situation—good or bad. She was like a Rock of Gibraltar for her daughter—strong, a guide, not easily moved. The Rock of Gibraltar marked the limit to the known world. To pass beyond it was to sail to certain destruction over the bottomless waterfall at the edge of the world.

Dr. Tonsmeyer told Sage, "Here are your options: One, you can have an abortion legally because you have a potentially dangerous and life-threatening situation to both you and the unborn child you carry. Or two, you can carry the child to term, and we can take the baby at thirty-six or thirty-seven weeks, which is two to three weeks short of a full-term, which has its dangers also."

"Are those the only two options?" Sage asked the doctor.

"Yes, there are only two," he said. "If you choose the first option, abortion, I can arrange for you to have it in Pensacola, Florida, because it is not legal in Alabama, and I cannot perform this surgical procedure because of my religious beliefs. If you choose to have the baby, Dr. Braun and I will do everything within our power medically to ensure you are well cared for during your pregnancy."

Dr. Tonsmeyer continued, "You do not have to make the decision today, but it has to be made before you enter the second trimester … Actually, I prefer you make it within the next ten days. Talk with your family. See what your husband's opinion is. By the way, where is he today?"

"At work. He did not think it was necessary to come," Sage said. She and the doctor let that part of the conversation drop.

After the visit to the doctor, Sage talked with her family. She also talked with each of her brothers and sisters on an individual basis: her sister Dysantha, who lived in Texas; her sister Victoria, who lived in Mobile; her brother Josef, who lived in Washington State (Sage had been his baby all her life); her brother Isaiah, who lived in Atlanta with her uncle and aunt; her brother Claybroune, who was married and lived locally; and her brother Marshall, who was married and lived locally. Sage lived up the fencerow from her parents, Jacque and Maria Seymour. She talked with her father and mother together.

Their comment to Sage was, "We are behind you whatever decision you make. We want you to make the decision based on what you feel. We are looking at two lives here—yours and your unborn child's. You are our baby, and we are talking about your baby. You have a healthy child, Charles, who needs his mother. We do not want you to jeopardize your life. If we have to choose, we want our baby to live and raise our grandchild. We don't know your unborn child, but we know you, and it would be hard to let you go."

Her brothers' and sisters' opinions mirrored her parents' views and opinions. They all wanted her to live and be healthy; they had already had her for a long time and did not want to lose her to death by childbirth or some little-known evil destructive disease.

Sage prayed the 121 Psalm of David, verses 1–8:

> *I will lift my eyes unto the hills, from whence comes my help. My help comes from the Lord, which made Heaven and Earth. He will not suffer m thy foot to be move; he that keepth thee will not slumber. Behold, He that keepth Israel shall neither slumber or sleep. The Lord is they keeper; the Lord is the shade upon my right hand. The sun shall not smite thee by day, nor the moon by night. The Lord shall preserve thee from all evil; he shall preserve thy soul. The Lord shall preserve they going out and they coming in for this time forth, and even for evermore.*

She prayed that the Lord would not forget her and hear her prayer, for she was a child before Him, His child. Isaiah 49:6 reminded Sage that the Lord said, "Can a woman forget her suckling child, that she should not have compassion on the son of her womb? Ye they may forget, yet I will not forget so quickly." Humans sometimes do not display care or concern for others. How easy it can be for humans to forget those in distress or in need.

> *Psalms 121:1–8: I will lift mine eyes unto the hills, from whence cometh my help. My help cometh from the Lord which made heaven and earth. He will not suffer thy foot to be moved: he that keepth thee will not slumber. Behold, he that keepeth Israel shall neither slumber of sleep.*
>
> *The Lord is they keeper; the Lord is they shade upon they right hand. The sun shall not smite thee by day, nor the moon by night. The Lord shall preserve thee from all evil: he shall preserve thy soul. The Lord shall preserve they going out and they coming in from this time forth, and even for evermore.*

Sage knew in her heart. Her mother had raised her to know that it is the nature of humans to forget, but God never forgets and neither is He late. His care and love is like a river that flows continually without ceasing. There are no dry seasons with the Father in heaven. Sage knelt before the throne of God and asked Him to grant her request to help her make the right decision about her pregnancy and to allow her to live to raise her unborn child. She held on to the belief that God was her refuge and strength, a very present help in the time of trouble (Ps. 46:1).

Sage's husband, Karl, didn't seem to consider her life or the life of their unborn child at risk. He wasn't able to grasp the seriousness of the situation. Sage knew he would not be any help to her in the hard and difficult decision she had to make; she didn't seem to have his support.

She felt as if she was talking to a stranger who had no interest or stake in the events that were unfolding in her and her family's lives. This change had a long arm, and it would have a far-reaching effect. It would bring about events that would change her life forever. Little did she realize that this was just the beginning of trouble and heartache for her and the entire Seymour family.

During the next ten days, Sage prayed constantly. The Scripture says to pray without ceasing (2 Thess. 5:17). Sage sought an answer to what she was to do, what road she should take. She meditated on what James 1:2–15 and Psalms 121 say about faith and not wavering in your belief that God will answer your prayer.

Psalms 46:1: God is my refuge and strength, a very present help in the time of trouble.

2 Thessalonians 5:17: Pray without ceasing.

Psalms 91:1–3: He that dwelleth in the secret place of the most high shall abide under the shadow of the Almighty. I will say of the Lord, He is my refuge and my fortress: my God in him will I trust. Surely he will deliver thee from the snare of the fowler, and from the noisome pestilence.

> *James 1:2–15: My brethren, count it all joy when you fall into diver's temptations; knowing this, that the trying of your faith worketh patience. But let patience have her perfect work, that ye may be perfect and entire, wanting nothing. If any of you lack wisdom, let him ask God, that giveth to all men liberally and upbraideth not; and it shall be given to him. But let him ask in faith, nothing wavering. For he that wavereth is like a wave of the sea driven with the wind and tossed. But let not that man think that he shall receive any thing of the Lord. A double minded man is unstable in all his ways. Let the brother of low degree rejoice in that he is exalted: But the rich, in that he is made low: because as the flower of the grass he shall pass away. For the sun is no sooner risen with a burning heat, but it withereth the grass, and the flower thereof falleth, and the grace of the fashion of it perisheth: so also shall the rich man fade away in his ways. Blessed is the man that endureth temptation: for when he is tried, he shall receive the crown of life, which the Lord hath promised to them that love him. Let no man sway when he is tempted, I am tempted of God: for God cannot be tempted with evil, neither tempteth he any man. But every man is tempted, when he is drawn away of his own lust and enticed. The when lust hath conceived it bringeth forth sin: and sin, when it is finished, bringeth forth death.*

After two weeks of prayer, Sage made a decision and talked with her mother about it. She decided she would go through with the pregnancy, put her faith and her situation in God's hands, and take her chances with the doctors. Sage knew she could die, but her fear of death was not as strong as her fear of aborting her baby; for her belief, like her doctors', would not allow her to take the life of her unborn child.

Sage saw her doctors and told them her decision. Dr. Tonsmeyer and Dr. Braun were overjoyed, for they too had been praying she would go through with the pregnancy. Dr. Tonsmeyer told her it did not mean that there would be no complications, but they would monitor her pregnancy and try to eliminate as many complications they could foresee as possible.

"Where is your husband today?" Dr. Tonsmeyer asked Sage.

"He is at work today," she said. "He did not think that he needed to here." Once again, both Dr. Tonsmeyer and Sage let the conversation drop.

Sage's pregnancy progressed well for the first six months—that is, in terms of the child. There were external complications, however; Sage's husband, Karl, was like a bull in a china shop. With the stretch of the imagination, anyone can imagine how a bull in a china shop would conduct himself. The word that came to Sage's mind was *destructive*, much like the disease that lived in her body.

As Sage pondered question the doctor asked each visit—"Where is your husband?"—she eventually discussed it with her mother and poured her heart about the fact that a wife is supposed to be part of her husband, and he is supposed to treat her as he would himself.

"Does not the Bible tell us this very point, Mother?" Sage asked.

"Yes, my dear, it does say that," her mother said.

"This scripture is found in Ephesians chapter five, verse twenty-five and twenty-eight through thirty-three," Sage said.

> *Ephesians 5: 25, 28–33: Husbands love your wives, even as Christ also loved the church, and gave himself for it. So men ought to love their wives as their own bodies. He that loveth his wife loveth himself. For no man ever yet hated his own flesh; but nourisheth and cherisheth it, even as the Lord does the church. For we are members of his body, of his flesh, and of his bones. For this cause a man should leave his father and mother, and shall be joined unto his wife, and they shall be one flesh. This is a great mystery: but I speak concerning Christ and the church. Nevertheless let every one of you in particular so love his wife even as himself; and the wife see that she reverence her husband.*

Sage ate a diet of fish and vegetables and only gained ten pounds over the course of the entire pregnancy. Her doctors told her that fresh veggies and fish would give her the nutrients she needed, along with other healthy protein and vitamins.

Sage's pregnancy continued to progress well until the seventh month. The seventh month brought a kidney infection that threatened the unborn child's life as well as Sage's. Sage was in the hospital for ten days as they administered fluids to get her kidneys functioning again. She went home, and the peace and good health lasted for three weeks. Then she was rushed to the doctor and then to the emergency room because of pain in her lower abdomen on her right side.

Sage was diagnosed with appendicitis. Her appendix was inflamed and getting worse. There were a lot of antibiotics she could take to help, but for fear of harming the baby boy, Doctors Tonsmeyer and Braun opted to give her the minimum antibiotics necessary. (The baby, by the way, was doing just fine).

"He is alive and kicking," Doctor Tonsmeyer said.

Even though her doctors tried to rally her spirits, Sage saw the worry and concern in their eyes and in the whispering to the nurses, the constant in and out of her hospital room, and the endless rushing around by both doctors and nurses. Even the nuns, the mother superior, and others came in to reassure Sage and Maria that everything was fine and that the hospital was giving the most careful and excellent care they could. Sage was more frightened than ever, and a sinking feeling engulfed her entire being.

"Don't give up on the doctors yet," her mother told her. "God will give them the wisdom and understanding they need to treat you. He has gotten them through seven months of treating you, and He won't let them or me down at this point" (Ps. 84:11).

Sage held on to her mother's words and her faith in God, which was all she had to hold on to. She knew prayer and belief moved mountains (Matt. 17:20–21).

> *Psalms 84:11: For the Lord God is sun and shield: the Lord will give grace and glory: no good thing shall he withhold from them that walk uprightly.*

> *Matthew 17:20-21: And Jesus said unto them: For verily I say unto you, "If you have faith as a grain of mustard seed, you shall say unto this mountain, Remove hence to yonder place; and it shall remove; and nothing shall be impossible for you. Howbeit this kind goeth not out but by prayer and fasting.*

Sage's husband may as well have been invisible; he offered no help or encouragement. The doctor gave Sage as much medication as her condition would allow. The hospital sent her home after ten days and ordered her to be on bed rest. She visited her doctors once a week so they could monitor her appendix. The doctors stood ready to take her unborn child at seven and a half months if necessary. They were on the lookout for signs that would determine whether or not they needed to take the baby, including a constant high fever, significant perspiration, a loss of appetite, and sharp continuous pain in her lower right abdomen.

Sage visited the doctors every week for the next four weeks; thankfully, the appendicitis had not progressed. The doctors were thankful but very cautious. During the last two weeks, Sage went to see the doctors every day. She drove herself, and her mother accompanied her to the doctor throughout the entire pregnancy. Sage attributed all blessing to the power of God; He did not heal the appendix, but He allowed her pregnancy to progress to full-term (which was thirty-seven weeks in her case) without the appendix bursting. Sage had been told that if it burst, there was a chance that she or the baby or both of them would be lost; the appendix would poison her entire system.

Sage's son was born at thirty-seven weeks by C-section. Chester Michael Jacobson was a perfect, 4 lb. boy with all his fingers, toes, eyes, ears, and a healthy set of lungs. He was born demanding attention. When she first saw him, Sage thought he was hardly larger than her hand; in fact, she could hold him in one hand.

Sage had a C-section, an appendectomy, and a partial hysterectomy all in one morning. Dr. Tonsmeyer and Dr. Braun were both in attendance at her son's birth that fine Monday morning on October 5, 1976.

After she awoke from anesthesia, Doctor Tonsmeyer told Sage that her inflamed appendix had not changed; it had been at the same stage it had been two and a half months earlier. And the malignant cancer on her uterus had not moved one centimeter in nine months. For Sage and her entire family, this was a day that was almost unbelievable, not to mention that they had never heard of someone carrying a baby to term under those conditions. Sage knew that God had answered her and her family's prayers.

Sage had made the "right" decision to carry her unborn child, even in the face of death and disease. She knew at that time that God could do anything and would not let her down in any situation. Dr. Braun and Dr. Tonsmeyer told Sage it was not necessary for her to take treatment for the malignant cancer because it had not progressed and all the danger had been removed. Sage did have to be checked every six months until her Pap smear tests were a category one again.

Sage had many blessings in her life: her family and friends but especially her mother, Maria, and her sister Dysantha, who had encouraged and supported her every step of that journey even though, at that time, Dysantha had cancer herself. The doctors thought her cancer was under control with the chemo treatments, but a few months later, it would prove to be false hope. Maria had been in Texas with Dysantha off and on for two to three years while she went through the chemo. She had come home for those few months to help take care of Sage, with the intent of going back to Texas to continue taking care of Dysantha.

Sage was thankful for her family, her life, and the chance to raise her children, but she was especially thankful for the greatest blessing of all—Chester Michael Jacobson.

He was a gift because under normal circumstances he would not have been born. Sage knew he had not been conceived under normal circumstances because of the cancer, and she had not carried him under normal circumstances. He was truly a gift from God. Actually, he was more than a gift; he was a miracle.

Sage felt as if she knew how Eve must have felt walking face-to-face and side-by-side with God each day. Sage too had walked in that spiritual garden with God in the cool of the day. She thought what a wonderful gift for Adam and Eve but especially Eve (Gen. 3:8).

When we as humans think of *a present*, we think of something that is given to us or something we get immediately. But when you think of *a gift*, it takes on a different meaning or connotation; *a gift* is something you receive or will receive that is lasting or that will have a lasting effect attached to it. The meaning of a gift is something that is given by somebody, usually in order to provide pleasure or to show gratitude. There can be a number of adjectives that describe a gift, but they are not the true meaning of the word itself.

Sage was and is a cancer survivor. The Bible describes a gift as a favor bestowed upon someone. God is the giver of every good and perfect, (James 1:17). God does not take away good gifts; He is true to His word (Num. 23:19). Sometimes man cannot or will not make good on his promise of gifts or keep his word. Gifts from God show man God's providence. The statement, Lo, children are a heritage from God" (Ps. 127:2) rings true.

Sage recalled what her grandmother, Elisha Barrington, said in a conversation they had about the number of sisters and brothers she had. Her grandmother told her, "Children are graciously given by God to humans." This biblical account made reference to Jacob upon his meeting his brother Esau twenty years after he stole Esau's birthright (Gen. 27:36; 33:6b).

> *Genesis 3:8: And they heard the voice of the Lord God walking in the garden in the cool of the day;*
>
> *James 1:17: Every good and every perfect gift cometh down from the father of light, with whom is no variableness, neither shadow of turning.*
>
> *Numbers 23:19: God is not a man that he should lie; neither the son of man that he should repent: hath he said, and shall he not do it? Or hath he spoken, and shall he not make it good*
>
> *Psalms 127:2 Ibid.*
>
> *Genesis 27.36: And he said, is not he rightly named Jacob? For he supplanted me these two times, he took away my*

birthright and behold he has taken away my blessing and he said, Hath though not reserved a blessing for me.

Genesis 33:6b: Then the handmaidens came near, they and their children, and thy lowed themselves.

Sage had been given three gifts at the birth of her son Chester. God had granted her two gifts of life and one gift of death. Sage and Chester's lives were the gift of life, and the death of only a part of Sage's body and not Sage herself was the third gift. God's providence and love are truly blessing and gifts; out of the many trials and tribulations over the seven and a half months of her pregnancy, Sage gained victory from a merciful and loving God.

Sage thought back to what her brother Claybroune used to tell their mother each time he walked in the woods as a child: "Mama, I saw something beautiful today." Sage knew she had seen and experienced something beautiful that fall day in October 1976.

There are many gifts man receives from God, both material and spiritual, but Sage knew she had received a gift of life from God. He had favored her with His providence. She had prayed that the Lord would not forget her and hear her prayer, for she was like a child before Him, His child. Sage was reminded what the Lord said about not forgetting His children (Isa. 49:6).

Man does forget so quickly. Humans sometimes do not display care or concern for others. How easy can is to forget those in distress or those in need. Sage's mother had raised her to know that it is the nature of humans to forget, but God never forgets, and neither is He late. His love and care is like a river that flows continuously without ceasing. There are no dry seasons with the Father in heaven.

Sage had knelt before the throne of God and asked Him to grant her request to help her make the right decision about her pregnancy and allow her to live to raise her unborn child. She held on to the belief that God was her refuge and strength, a very present help in the time of trouble, (Ps. 46:11).

Little did Sage know that these joyous times would only last for a short while; in January of 1977, clouds of despair and grief would move in and stay with the Seymour family for years. The hurricane rushed in, the eye of the storm sat over the Seymour family, the winds blew, and the rain poured in.

> *Isaiah 49:6: God said, "Can a woman forger her suckling child, that she should have compassion on the son of her womb? Yea, thy may forget, yet I will not forget thee.*

> *Psalms 46:11: God is my refuse and strength, a very present help in the time of trouble.*

Chapter 2

The Hurricane Rushes In

Dysantha was in Austin, Texas, the entire time she had cancer. The radiation and chemotherapy ravaged her body as much as the disease. She suffered enormous pain in the wake of these treatments. The radiation affected the color and moisture of her skin. She lost her hair, which had once hung down her back to her waistline. She lost it to the extent that it became boyish in length.

In the 1970s, cancer treatments were not as advanced as they are today; therefore, the lack of knowledge of more advanced treatments proved to be costly for Dysantha. Like Sage, the cancer started in her uterus. A few years before, she'd had a test that revealed the cancerous cells were there. In her desire to have a child, she opted to have her uterus frozen at the doctor's suggestion. But when she got pregnant, the hormonal changes seem to wake the cancer cells up, and they moved through her bloodstream to her mouth.

She chose to bring the baby into the world at the risk of her own life. Unlike Sage, her cancer moved through her bloodstream during the hormonal changes during her pregnancy. Dysantha left a baby boy. Marchus Edmonds was a beautiful baby boy and became an even more handsome man.

Sage said, "He grew up to be a picture of that symmetry of art, with that diamond quality that is inherent in the Seymour-Barrington descendants. He is a fine gentlemen, well bred, and successful."

When Dysantha began taking treatments, the chemotherapy caused the cells to move to her mouth. The movement of the cancer cells also resulted in Dysantha losing her jawbone. She was fitted for prosthesis after doctors removed the jawbone. The surgery changed Dysantha. Her face was sunken in on one side. This had a great effect on her mental state. She essentially went into a state of hiding. When she was in the public, she wore a scarf over her face. She was no longer the confident and enthusiastic person she had once been. Instead, she was withdrawn and shy in public. Even when she came to see her family, she would shy away.

Sage remembered the first time she saw her sister after her surgery. Dysantha hid her face with a scarf. She arrived at Sage's front door with the scarf in place over her face.

"Hello, pet," Dysantha said.

Sage was so overcome with emotion that she could hardly speak. "Hello, Dysantha," she said, "I'm glad to see you."

In her heart, Sage was glad to see her sister because she loved her with all her heart, but in her mind she could not bear the pain she saw as she looked at her sister. She saw a once beautiful, vibrant, young woman who had been so full of vitality reduced by this evil disease to a frail, small, almost unrecognizable person. *This cannot be my sister who was so beautiful and graceful,* thought Sage.

Her heart and emotions were locked in a battle with the love she felt for her sister and the fear of seeing her in this frail condition, with her right jawbone and teeth gone. On her face was an ugly scar where her jawbone and teeth had been removed. Dysantha's natural skin color had been like peaches and cream; the radiation had left her with a dark, scaly look on one side of her face. She looked as if the radiation had been overdone.

Dysantha stayed with Sage for a few days while she visited her family in Chunchula. Sage could barely look at her sister during her visit. The guilt she felt did not help the situation any. So overcome with emotion, Sage frequently went into her bedroom and cried unmercifully. Why she could not figure it out? Was it because of the guilt she felt because of the fact that her sister was not the same, or was it because Sage was afraid Dysantha might die?

Sage realized that it was because of none of those reasons; it was because she desperately wanted to help her sister, and she realized there was nothing she could do. She was at the mercy of God. But Sage felt as if God had not helped her sister. Dysantha was a smart, kind, caring, and loving sister. She was an angel to Sage. Why would God allow this to happen to her sister? There were so many terrible people in the world that did not face assault on any level. Why were good people the ones who were subjected to cruel diseases that ravaged their bodies? Sage prayed for an answer and a cure for her sister. But no answer came, and her sister grew worse. God had deserted her in her darkest hour.

Sage prayed for her sister as hard as she could, but these prayers were unheard and to no avail. Sage became very angry with everyone and everything. Dysantha was so young at twenty-seven years of age. The hurricane had rushed in with a force under which Sage was unable to stand. The pressure was too great. The pain was unbearable. Her emotions were out of control. Her thoughts were not rational, and she felt completely lost. She was in a dark cave, and a grizzly stood at the entrance.

The cold, harsh winds of change blew relentlessly across the lives of the Seymour family. Like the first chill of fall, the cruel winds of death lingered for many a season, just like a guest that stays longer than wanted.

Chapter 3

The Gentle Breeze

Texas is not a great distance from Alabama if someone you love and cherish lives there and has a possibly terminal disease. Ovarian cancer, uterine cancer, or any other form of this destructive disease was not as well known, curable, or researched in the 1970s as it is today. But to Sage, her sister seemed as if she was a million miles away rather than a few hours.

When Dysantha called Sage and told her she had cancer and that it had moved through her bloodstream to her mouth, Sage had felt like someone had turned out the lights. She was thrown on a mental and emotional roller coaster. Numbness set in, and she turned to God and began to hope and pray that her sister would recover.

Sage's mind went back to four years before when she had visited her sister in Austin. The time they spent together left pleasant memories that would last for a lifetime. At that time her sister had been so full of life, without a hint of trouble or illness on the horizon. Sage could see her sister's pleasant smile, hear her soft voice, and remember her kind spirit.

Now Dysantha seemed a million miles away. Sage wanted to be near her sister and support her, but she did not know how to give support or know what her sister needed. She was still so young, and her parents had sheltered her from the world, trouble, and hurt; therefore, she didn't know what path to take. This was one she had not traveled before. Fear of the unknown had a very debilitating effect on her. She felt as if she was bound by the chains of time and distance. She had no wiggle room.

Sage was beset with fear and dread of the possible future for her sister; the situation felt hopeless, and she felt helpless. Sage's mother, Maria, had always been her best friend, the person with whom she discussed everything, no matter how large or small the problem or issue. But the tables had turned, and Sage knew somehow she would need to be the strong shoulder for her mother and father both to lean on. But how?

Sage's father, Jacque Seymour, was like still waters that run deep. He was strong and sturdy as an oak. He had always been a loving and kind father, faithful and always there for his family. He was a quiet man and did not express his love for his family verbally, but he showed his family that he loved them.

Sage worried about her father and wondered if he would be all right when he heard the news about his middle daughter and the terrible disease that was ravishing her body. He was the type of man that felt deeply, and this type of pain would tear at his heart and mind. Sage recognized her father's reaction to pain and hurt; he would swing his crossed left leg back and forth, drop his head, and close his eyes as if he could shut out the pain this way, but she knew he could not, for Jacque loved his children with all of his being.

In contrast, her mother was sturdy and strong, with very intense feelings; she loved her children with the same fervency that Jacque did, but unlike him, she did not keep her feeling hidden. Maria's way of handling this type of pain included tears, noticeable irritation, and shortness in patience, when under normal circumstances she was the most patient and kind soul Sage had ever known—that is, unless she was backed against a wall.

Sage wondered how she and her family would deal with this overwhelming situation, especially herself. She lived up the fence row from her parents, as they said in the country, and she was with her parents daily. As the months and years went by, the bond they shared grew even stronger.

Over a progression of months, Sage saw her sister begin to succumb to the effects of the disease. She was like a fading rose. Little by little, piece by piece, Dysantha began to fade away. The rose that had always thrived, so full of life, and had brought so much beauty into Sage and her family's life was undergoing a change that would leave a void for a long time.

Sage saw herself reaching for her sister, but it was as though she was a mirage; the closer Sage got to her, the more the mirage faded until eventually it was not there anymore. Sage knew that just as the mirage had faded into eternity, so would her sister Dysantha.

On an unforgettable day in April 1977, Dysantha faded from this world.

Dysantha was a gentle breeze that blew through Sage's life, gone too soon after twenty-seven years of life. Sage could not bear the heavy burden of her sister's untimely death—taken by an evil, unrelenting disease that destroys. What a challenge for Sage—a painful challenge. Tears hurt even more. How could Sage bear this loss? She felt as if her heart had been torn from her chest; her mind swirled with questions.

Where was God? How could He allow her sister to be taken so soon? Left with a void in her life, Sage became angry and bitter. While Dysantha been living and suffering terrible, unspeakable pain, Sage had unceasingly sought God prayerfully on her sister's behalf but to no avail. Why would He take this precious sister from her?

Few people Sage met had the qualities of a precious jewel. Dysantha had sparkled and helped bring beauty into the lives of everyone with whom she came in contact.

Sage prayed for understanding of why her sister was taken. Cancer was an unforgiving disease—destructive and debilitating. Though the disease had destroyed the physical beauty of Dysantha, the beauty Sage remembered about her sister was of a spiritual nature, which no physical disease could touch.

This devastating time brought about a change in Sage that would last for years. She turned from God; He had abandoned her when she was in a dark valley with no light to guide her. In Sage's bitterness, she became selfish and hard-hearted. God did not care. He didn't answer prayers. It was a waste of time asking for His help.

On the outside, Sage wore a different garment for the world to see; she was friendly to the world and considered the world as her friend. But inwardly she wore a spiritual garment of bitterness. The world did not see Sage's bitterness because the world had become Sage's friend instead of God. The world saw a different Sage than who she really was. She wore her garment of smiles, laughter, joy, and agreement. But with God, she was in a constant battle of the spirit; unlike the garment she wore for the world, she was naked in spirit before God, with no hope, no faith.

In reflection, Sage knew she was playing the true hypocrite because she was two different people. She compared her personality to the Dr. Jekyll/Mr. Hyde syndrome: in the light and with the world she was loving and happy, but in the dark and inwardly she was at war with God. Peter had played the hypocrite with the Jews and Gentiles. Before the Jews, he acknowledged Jesus; before the Gentiles he denied Christ. According to Mark 14:67–68, Peter was told: "Thou wast with Jesus of Nazareth." But he denied, saying, "I know not, neither understand what thou sayeth."

Sage described her feeling of friendship with the world through Paul Laurence Dunbar's poem, "We Wear the Mask" (2010).

We Wear the Mask

We wear the mask of grins and lies,
It hides our cheeks and shades our eyes,—
This debt we pay to human guile;
With torn and bleeding hearts we smile,
And mouth with myriad subtleties.

Why should the world be over-wise?
In counting all our tears and sighs?
Nay, let them only see us, while
We wear the mask.

We smile, but, O great Christ, our cries
To thee from tortured souls arise,
We sing, but oh the clay is vile
Beneath our feet, and long the mile;
But let the world dream otherwise,
We wear the mask!

Sage wore a mask before the world, but she smiled while her heart was breaking as she grew angrier and angrier with God. In the battle she waged with God, she discovered years later that she had always been outnumbered. God did not need her; she needed Him since He was the giver of all things.

After Dysantha's death, Sage felt as if she was trapped in a cave with a grizzly bear blocking the entrance. She had no way out. The grizzly symbolized death and her inability to help her sister in her most desperate hour. She could not forgive herself for her inability to provide the comfort and support her sister had needed. She realized she had run away into a dark cave to hide so she would not have to look at the devastation the evil disease had caused. She did not want any light; the comfort of darkness was her friend.

Fear of the light and the inevitable stood like a grizzly at the entrance of the cave. Sage had known her sister would not overcome the evil monster and that she would lose her. It was unbearable. Sage could not face it.

Until Sage's sister, death had not been reality to her. It was an illusion, a mirage. Sage had believed her sister would get better and would not die. In the desert, that had seemed real but it was too far off to tell. But the closer Sage had gotten to the mirage, the more it had become a reality; the desert spring was not there, and there was no hope for survival from the unforgiving heat. Sage had known there was no hope for her sister.

Sage's heart was permanently scarred—an ugly keloid scar that served as a constant reminder of the pain and suffering of the loss in her life. Sage told me that she thought of a time years earlier when she was cooking dinner for her husband and children and she cut herself on the oven door.

When she cooked, she wore an oversized T-shirt. The stove in her kitchen was typical: white, thirty-six inches wide, four cooking eyes. The oven door had an aluminum handle with sharp edges. Sage recalled the oven was hot, and as she passed, she got a little too close, and it burned her leg. In her effort to avoid being burned seriously, she moved quickly, and the upper part of her thigh hit the tip of the oven door, which cut a gash in her leg.

She bled for some time, and after the wound was cleaned and bandaged, it burned for a while. She noticed a few days later that the wound was healing, but there was something different about this healing; the scar had immediately keloid even before the wound completely healed, and it had become an ugly, unforgettable scar. Every time she looks at her leg, she is reminded of the incident. The scar still itches; even years later, the healing process is not complete.

Sage related this incident to the scars on her heart; those scars have not completely healed either. And like the keloid on her leg, the ones on her heart are just as ugly. Even though they heal, outward scars seldom disappear; likewise, inward scars seldom disappear inwardly even though they heal.

Scars stand as vigilant watchmen—a constant reminder of the pain and suffering that caused them But in contrast to the scar on Sage's thigh, the scar on her heart has not healed properly.

Trying to change her perspective on her sister's untimely death and her relationship with God would prove to be a daunting task; she was not outfitted emotionally to climb this mountain to try to find healing. She was certain it wasn't going to happen. She could remain bitter; it was the path of least resistance.

Chapter 4

The Fading Rose

Roses are one of the most beautiful flowers in the world. Sage remembered her mother's love for roses. She had rose gardens in several areas of her landscaping. Red roses, yellow roses, and pink roses all lined the yard. People came from miles around just to look at Maria's yard and flower gardens.

Maria had a green thumb for making things grow, whether they were flowers, children, or vegetables. Sage remembers how her mother fertilized her roses with cow chips from the pasture or chicken droppings from the chicken yard. She worked constantly on her yard each day. The efforts she put into her yard and flower garden, as well as the efforts she put into her children, all paid off.

Sage remembered picking roses as a child and putting them in a pint jar full of water (vases were scarce, unheard of, or nonexistent) and put them on the kitchen table or in the girls' rooms to brighten the rooms up a little. She would change or replenish the water as needed or when Maria told her she needed to. But after four or five days, the rose blossoms would start to wither around the edges. The withering would then progress to the entire petals, and they would fall off the stem one by one until they were all gone.

Though the rose petals were beautiful, they could not live detached from the stem, and the stem could not survive detached from the roots. The fading process of the roses continued until they were gone completely. Sage compared her sister Dysantha with one of the most beautiful flowers in the world—the rose.

Sage had not witnessed each stage in the progression of Dysantha's cancer, but she had known her sister was fading away little by little. There had been no chance of her survival. Each stage of her sister's cancer, Sage compared to the petals falling from a rose. The outer edges started to wither, and ultimately the entire rose faded and withered with time.

Sage said, "Dysantha was like this beautiful rose because she was as beautiful as a rose in full bloom." Dysantha had been kind, empathetic, sweet, caring, understanding, and loving. She had stood out wherever she went; she had always been positive and uplifting, just as a rose is when someone looks at it.

Roses are given for many reasons. They are given for love, recognition, achievement—the list goes on and on. Roses say *special*. That was what Dysantha was—*special*. Dysantha had been loaned by God to the Seymour family for just twenty-seven short years. It was a short-term loan for such a precious sister.

Before her sister's death, it seemed to Sage that Dysantha's life had just started to blossom. She had been a social worker at one of the major hospitals in Austin, Texas. She had been as loved by her peers there, as she was by anyone with whom she came in contact. Dysantha had been a hard worker who had been a delight to her family and people around her. She had left a trail of joy and peace everywhere she went. Dysantha, like a rose, had faded so fast that it was a shock to the Seymour family; it had felt as if the life was being sucked out of them all little by little. As the months and weeks had passed, Dysantha had faded a little more each day, with no possibility of her being healthy again.

Chapter 5

The Dilemma

Sage's mother was a remarkable woman. Sage remembered the sacrifices her mother had made for her family while they were young; she had gone without on many occasions so that her family could have the bare necessities in life.

Three years before the family knew Dysantha was ill, Sage had noticed her mother had begun to be quieter than usual and her face had a worried look on it each time she saw and talked with her. It was difficult to see her mother in such a state. Sage asked Maria to tell her what was worrying her. She knew her mother had gone to the doctor several times. Since those visits, Maria had become distant, and the pain that came from it was unbearable for Sage. Sage knew she had not offended her mother in any way, but she could not figure out the problem and the reason for distance.

Maria finally confessed to Sage that she was ill and the doctor had given her some bad news: she had cancer. Sage was silent for a whole hour before she could respond. She just sat and looked into space and wondered if she had heard her mother wrong. Sage thought back to a few years before when her sister had first became ill. Maria had gone to Texas and cared for Dysantha for about three years. Sage realized that her mother had known that she was sick when she was in Texas; she had known she had cancer.

Maria's cancer had progressed too far; it had reached stage three the few months she had been back home from Texas before Dysantha's death. Maria had returned home in September 1976 to care for Sage. While there, she had visited Dr. Braun and Dr. Tonsmeyer for a physical exam. (Sage had known then that her mother had cancer the entire time she cared for her during her pregnancy and after her baby was born). Maria left in November to go back to Texas, but she only stayed a month. Upon her return, Maria had another Pap smear; the test results showed the disease had reached stage three—as bad as it could get at that time.

Dr. Braun and Dr. Tonsmeyer scheduled an exploratory procedure for Maria to determine the extent of the cancer. The week before the procedure in January 1977 felt like an eternity. The day finally arrived, and Maria went to Providence Hospital on Springhill Avenue for the procedure.

It was no time before the doctors were back in the lobby to speak with the family. Sage thought it was a quick turn-around. The family's hope rose because they thought it was good news. However, with the doctors' visit to the family came even more devastating news: the cancer was not only in her ovaries, but it had spread to every organ of her body. When Maria was opened up, the air only made the cancer spread even faster. Dr. Braun and Dr. Tonsmeyer could not do anything for her; they could only close the incision and do their best to treat the evil disease.

Maria started chemotherapy, which was not as effective then as it is today. The knowledge of effective treatment for cancer was not very advanced in the 1970s. Maria went home, where she was treated on a weekly basis. During the first month, she lost all of her long, beautiful hair. She lost weight, and her appetite changed almost by the minute. One minute she was hungry, and the next minute she was not.

February brought a very trying time for the Seymour family. Just the knowledge that both mother and sister had cancer that started in their uteruses or their ovaries and had engulfed their entire bodies was more than their minds could comprehend. March was even worse. Dysantha had grown worse by this point; the radiation treatment was burning her alive. Maria not only grieved because she could not be with her daughter but also because she knew that she was also fading fast.

Maria was not able to care for Dysantha anymore. April 1977 brought even more pain. A call came from Dysantha's husband Herman. He said Dysantha had been taken to the hospital in Dallas and had slipped into unconsciousness. Victoria, Claybroune, Marshall, and several other family members went to Texas to see her. They arrived just in time; Dysantha had hung on until they arrived. She responded to the knowledge that her family was there, even though she was unconscious. Dysantha passed from this life a few hours later.

Sage could not bear to go see her sister for the last time; she wanted to remember her as she had been. Maria could not go, though she seemed a little stronger. Jacque hardly spoke during this entire time. He sat with his eyes closed and his head hung down. What pain must have been invading his thoughts and heart? He was losing his beautiful daughter, and his precious Maria was so sick; it was a lot to bear all at once. Even in her illness, Maria was remarkably strong mentally. She kept her family pulled together through the services for Dysantha and even afterward.

In May, Maria's health started to go downhill again. Fluid had started gathering in her body; she went to the hospital for it to be drawn off at least once a week. Even more than the fluid, she started passing large chunks of flesh. The entire summer of 1977 was an ordeal for the whole family. In September, Maria's health started failing fast. She became bedridden the last two weeks of September 1977. In October 5, 1977, an ambulance was called to the Seymour home; she was taken to Providence, but on the way she drowned in her own fluid. The doctor said fluid had covered her heart and lungs.

Sage remembered her mother when she was being taken out to the ambulance by the medics. She had seemed unconscious and unaware of her surroundings. Jacque could not go to the hospital; he waited at home to hear the news. He knew she would never return to their home again.

Sage had cooked her mother her last meal. She had wanted fried chicken, so Sage rushed home and fried the chicken, and then took it to her. She had enjoyed the few bites she ate. Sage had stayed with her mother all evening that dreary day in October 1977. She had talked to her mother about many things. Her mother had told her one of the reasons she hated dying was because of Sage. She wished she had not sheltered her so much.

"You are my baby girl, and you seem so vulnerable and innocent," she had told Sage.

Sage asked her mother why she had not gotten treatment for the evil disease all the years before Sage had gotten pregnant, when Maria had gone to Texas to take care of Dysantha.

Maria had told her that when faced with the dilemma of caring for herself or caring for her daughters who needed her, she had chosen to care for her children rather than herself. "I have lived a great part of my life. Y'all still had yours to live; therefore, I chose your lives over mine. I do not regret my decision one moment. I am your mother, and I love you."

Her mother's act had been one of total unselfishness. "My mother's love was dependable, endless, strong, tender, kind, warm, friendly, and enduring. What a great legacy or gift to leave a daughter," Sage said.

That was the last conversation Sage had with her mother. The Seymour family buried their precious Maria on October 12, 1977—seven months to the day from when they buried their sister Dysantha. Death is a fierce enemy to overcome. More pain beset Sage and her family. Sage did not know where to turn at this point.

Chapter 6

The Grizzly

A grizzly is a ferocious animal that stands nine feet tall, with claws that can destroy and rip apart any prey he battles. A grizzly hugs his prey. He can literally crush it to death with his enormous strength. A grizzly's long molars (teeth) can literally tear the head off a body.

A grizzly at the entrance of the cave was how Sage described her feelings about her sister's illness. The cancer was ferocious, with claws that tore at her emotions. The pain from the tears caused a ripple effect that reached all the way to her soul.

How does a human fight a grizzly? He is bigger, more powerful, and has the power to destroy. Like the grizzly, her sister's cancer had destroyed Sage's emotions, confidence, faith, and strength. She did not know how to fight these feelings, which reached so deeply and gripped her entire being with unbearable pain.

The darkness of the cave gave Sage the cover she needed to avoid facing the reality of the beginning of the tragedy that was about to beset her family.

Truthfully, Sage was glad for the grizzly at the entrance of the cave. For a while it allowed her to feel peace in the dark of the cave, because light would have allowed her to see the destruction of the evil disease that was destroying her sister.

At that time, there was no one to rescue her from this painful dilemma, as there is no rescuer from the attack of a grizzly. A grizzly destroys his prey quickly. By the time a rescuer arrives (i.e., better treatment for the cancer was found) the damage was done; her sister and mother were gone.

Sage wondered if there would ever come a time when there would be a complete cure for cancer. It attacked like a thief in the night. No one can know when a thief has it in his or her heart and mind to make an unwanted entrance. Thieves send no warning or announcement that they will be coming to take, destroy, or kill. They can take away a good part of your life. It is just the same with cancer. It has no warning signs. It just starts and is discovered afterward, not before. It too takes away a good part of your life. In its wake, cancer leaves a trail of destruction, pain, and heartache. There are different reasons why cancer starts, but these causes were not as well known in the 1970s as they are now.

Sage had to find a road back to the beginning of her anger and distance from God. Where could she begin? How could she begin? Which way would she go? What road should she take? She was still lost after the fog of pain and heartache started to clear …

Chapter 7

The Pain in Loving

Because we are angry at God does not mean He is going to go away. As she suffered hurt and anger, Sage had shut off her feelings; she stopped allowing herself to feel the love and passion she had once felt for her family and her loved ones.

She was in a very dark place for many years after her sister and mother died within less than a year of each other. Life had become useless and overwhelming. Forgotten was the joy and love she had for life and her family. Sage turned inward. Her heart ached because of the tremendous loss she had suffered.

Where had God been when she needed Him? Where was He? Why had He abandoned her and her family?

Sage watched her father suffer after her sister's death and during the next few months preceding her mother's death. Too much tragedy had beset the family at one time.

Maria had always been the center of her family. Everything about the family's life had resolved around Mom. She was that sturdy tree, and her children were like flowers blooming around the trunk. What would become of the strong bond that had been in the family so many years? It seemed as if it was falling apart.

Love for Sage was too painful. Trying to make sense of the losses was even more painful. So Sage shut out all thoughts to the point of almost refusing to acknowledge that she and her family had suffered great losses. Death had always been something that happened to someone else; even when her grandmother, Elisha Barrington, died when she was nineteen, Sage had known she was gone, but it did not bother her the way her sister's and mother's deaths did. At the time of Sage's grandmother's death, she had been so young and very sheltered and untouched by life and the world. Life should not be this difficult for anyone. But the shelter was gone now! Maria was gone!

Sage knew the Scripture said, "Man is a sojourner on their way to a city whose founder and maker is God" (Heb. 10:11). But this meaning eluded her at that time. Sage had been taught the Scripture so well by her grandmother. She had always heard that change was good. But what good could come out of pain and hurt? There was no answer for this question for her.

After all, God had turned His back on her, and she had distanced herself from God and her family and her loved ones in an effort to prevent any further pain and suffering. The loss of her most beloved sister and precious mother was too much for her to handle.

Sage went through the motions of living for a long time. There did not seem to be any light no matter where she turned. She could not focus on the positive side of life because of all the dark places that inhabited her life. Darkness came to visit and never seemed to leave.

Darkness is defined as things that are hidden from view; what is obscure or difficult to perceive or penetrate; an impending storm filling the atmosphere with gloom; ignorance (naiveté and inexperience); dimness of discernment (no distinctness to life that can be discerned); obscurity of reasoning (no understanding, lacks insight). Sage suffered all these things while in darkness. When a storm comes, there are always signs that it is on its way. The winds blow, the rain falls, and the clouds are dark, which causes the environment to look dark and hazy and makes visibility difficult. The impending storm had begun to rage long before her sister's and mother's deaths.

Sage was naïve and inexperienced; her power of discernment was one of a child wandering in the dark. She did not have understanding at this period in her life; she lacked insight or reasoning. Pain causes irrational thoughts and actions in humans, especially when it is pain associated with loving a child, a parent, or a sibling. Sage had suffered the loss of all three. Sage was the child (she had lost sight of herself), her mother was the parent, and her sister was the sibling. This type of pain is almost unbearable, especially when you have little experience with life and death. Up to this point in her life, Sage had not had experience with either. She lost herself and her reasoning. She wandered about in a fog, with no direction or understanding.

Sage's journey back to herself and back to God begins ... Her thoughts go back to the times before her mother and sister died ...

> *Hebrews 11:10: For he looked for a city which hath foundations, whose builder and maker is God.*

Chapter 8

The Long Way Home

Sage felt as though she had come to a crossroads in her life and taken the wrong path. She knew she could not take the same road all the way back to the beginning of the long two-year journey she had been on. She used the poem "The Road Not Taken" by Robert Frost to describe the feeling, but she expressed to me that she would need to take that same road back to where it had diverged in the yellow wood, which now seemed a lifetime ago. When Sage arrived at the crossroads, it still wanted wear; still the road less traveled or not taken.

The pain of losing a loved one never goes away, but it lessens in time. Only through God is this type of agony manageable. Sage meditated on Psalms 91: "He that dwelleth in the secret of the most high shall abide under the shadow of the almighty until these calamities be overpassed." God's shoulders are big enough and strong enough to handle any situation. Sage remembered that God gave His only begotten Son to die for a sinful world. Jesus's sacrifice conquered death and gave mankind hope for an eternity with God.

Psalms 91: He that dwelleth in the secret of the most high shall abide under the shadow of the almighty. I will say of the Lord; He is my refuse and my fortress, My God: In Him will I trust. Surely He shall deliver thee from the snare of the fowler, and from the non-some pestilence.

He shall cover thee with his feather and under his wing shall thou trust; His truth shall be thy shield and buckler. Thou shall not be afraid for the terror by night; nor the arrow that flieth by day; nor for the pestilence that walketh neither in the darkness, nor for the destruction that waseth at noonday. Because he hast made the Lord; which is my refuse, even the most high thy habitation. There shall be no evil befall thee neither shall any plague come nigh they dwelling.

God answers and says: "Because he has set his love upon me, therefore will I deliver him: I will set him on high, because he hath known my name. He shall call upon me, and I will answer him: I will be with him in trouble; I will deliver him and honor him. With long life will I satisfy him and show him my salvation.

Psalms 91 was one of Sage's favorite passages in the Bible. She focused on the words of this prayer to help her get through this difficult time.

Sage felt God had deserted her in her deepest hour of need. She could not see the way. She related her feeling of desertion to standing and looking at one set of footprints in the sand. Parents don't desert their children. She was a child of God. Why had the Heavenly Father deserted her?

He had been with her during her pregnancy and delivery; she'd had a healthy baby boy. Why desert her during her sister's and then her mother's illnesses. Cancer is such an evil, debilitating disease; it destroys not just your body but your emotions and peace of mind.

As her mind cleared, she began to see her journey but could only one set of footprints in the sand; earlier in her life, there had always been two. As she continued to look, she noticed the footprints were large, too large for her feet. They appeared to be man-sized prints. For the first time she realized that they were the prints of her Lord and Savior. All during the deepest hours of despair, confusion, anger, abandonment, heartache, pain, and feelings of desertion, Jesus had carried her the entire time. She thought about the poem "Footprints in the Sand."

As she worked through her feelings, each of these trials presented a challenge and was more emotional than any other feelings. But as she reflected back that to what Chinese philosopher Lao Tzu (604–531 BC) said about a journey, a long journey: "The journey of a thousand miles begins with one step." Sage compared the journey with walking toward the mountain—a still reminder of the awesomeness of God.

Like Adam and Eve in the Garden of Eden, we are naked before God; there is no way to cover up. We can cover our physical bodies but not our spiritual bodies. During the deepest, darkest, most difficult part of this journey, Sage had painted her physical house, trimmed it well, decorated the yard for all to see with the physical eye, but she forgot that God looks past the physical body to see the spiritual body only. According to Jeremiah 17:10, "God looks, and searches our hearts and our minds."

Pretty decorations are important to man but not God. Smiles and laughter were prevalent in Sage's life, but as a flower withers for lack of care, so did her soul and spirit. There was no hope, only despair, but all the time Sage was closer to God than ever before. He is our Father, and he knows and sees our pain and heartaches. Matthew 11:28–30 tells us of Jesus's invitation to "Come to me all ye that labor and are heavy laden and I will give you rest. Take my yoke upon you, learn of me, for I am meek and lowly in heart and ye shall find rest for your souls. For my yoke is easy, and my burdens is light."

Sage had questioned God, but like Job, she came to the realization that no man can question God (Job 40:1–8). He has the questions and the answers for man. He is the potter, and we are the clay. He molds and makes us after His will, not we our own (Isa. 64:8).

Job 40:1–8: Moreover, the Lord answered Job, and said, shall he that contendeth with the Almighty instruct him? he that reproveth God, let him answer it. Then Job answered the Lord, and said, Behold, I am vile; what shall I answer thee? I will lay mine hand upon my mouth. Once have I spoken; but, I will not answer; yea, twice; but I will proceed no further. Then answered the Lord unto Job out of the whirlwind, and said, Gird up thy loins now like a man: I will demand of thee, and declare thou unto me. Wilt thou also disannul my judgement? Wilt thou condemn me, that thou mayest be righteous?

Isaiah 64:8: But now, O Lord, thou are our father; we are the clay, and thou our potter; and we all are the work of thy hands.

The answer to Sage's mother's and sister's suffering and deaths can be found in Jesus's suffering and death. All that come to God must take the path that Jesus took. Also, Sage remembered that Satan is our adversary; he destroys. Until Christ comes for us again, trouble, suffering, and death will be part of life because Satan is still alive and well. He is the god of this world and is in battle with God for our souls. He destroys what he can—our physical bodies. He cannot destroy our souls unless we allow him to. God was with Sage all the time. Mountains do not move, and neither does God our Father. He is there always, standing strong and tall.

Sage knew that she must search for God with her heart, not her eyes. For there is hopelessness in a search for God with human eyes; man must search for God with his heart through obedience. Obedience to God is where hope lies, unmolested and waiting to make its home within our souls, where only God can dwell.

Chapter 9

Straddling the Fence

Sage had straddled the fence long enough. She was a farm girl. Her father fenced in their property to keep his livestock from roaming. To make sure the horses, mules, and cows did not leave the pasture, he stretched two rows of barbwire across the top. Barbwire has prongs on it, and if you are not careful, you can damage some parts of your person on it. Or if the wire breaks, it would painfully wrap you in it.

Climbing over the barbwire or getting between the rows of wire is a painstaking journey. The fence under the barbwire is just regular fencing wire; it is tough and strong and has square holes in it. This wire is safe to climb or straddle, but not the barbwire; it will cause enormous amounts of pain and suffering.

Sage compared her life to the barbwire fence. The bottom half of the fence was safe; that is God's way. The barbwire, with its prongs and ability to cut, maim, and lame her was the world. There is nothing in the world; as stated in a John 2:16: All that is in the world is the lust of the flesh, the lust of the eye, and the pride of life.

The bottom part of the fence Sage compared to God. He is always there, and we can get Him any time, day or night. He is always there for His children. The door to God, like the fencing wire, is always open; He never closes the door to salvation while we are here on Earth.

But straddling the wire is pain in and of itself. One can hardly get across barbwire without doing some damage. Trying to be friends with or getting to know the world can also result in pain and suffering.

Christ said in Revelations 3:15–16 that He wishes that they were either hot or cold—He would spew you out of His mouth. It is disgusting to Him when we can't make up our minds about which side of the fence we want to be on—world or Kingdom. So we straddle the fence, trying to live in both worlds.

Sage had not even straddled the fence; she went over the barbwire to the other side, suffering damage to her as a person as she went.

> *1 John 2:16: All that is in the world is the lust of the flesh, the lust of the eye, and the pride of life.*

> *Revelations 3:15–16: I know thy works, that thou are neither cold nor hot: I would thou wert cold or hot. So then because thou art lukewarm, and neither cold or hot, I will spue thee out of my mouth.*

The journey back across that fence to the other side posed the same pain but in a different way. She had to face God. This was a daunting task. Facing the world is easy; you are just part of the crowd. The crowd moves one way; therefore, if you go with the flow, you fit right in. There is no difference.

But when facing God, there is no crowd. God judges and deals with each of us on an individual basis. Jeremiah 17:10 says, I God search the heart and gives to each man according to his doings. He deals with each of His children differently but by the same rule of thumb. His commandments do not change. God decides the type and extent of punishment that should or should not be given to each of His children, just as earthly parents do for their children. They don't punish each child the same. But if one deed or transgression is punishable by the same rule of thumb, so will be all deeds and transgressions.

Sage knew she had to cross the fence again and face the music of her choice. When she arrived back at the fence, she stood with the barbwire she had once straddled years before. She looked and mused to herself about how she had allowed herself to get so far off track. Pain blinds us, as does love; she suffered both in the loss of her loved ones.

Chapter 10

The Journey Begins

Humans have the idea of what perfection is in terms of an individual professing Christianity. According to the Bible in Acts 11:26: And the disciples were called Christians first in Antioch. Second Timothy 1:1–7 states: Christians are people of Christ; the Called Out. Sage thought of the warfare taking place between the people of God and the servants of Satan. War is always the most deadly game a human can imagine. Just as soldiers of all kinds and from all walks of life are called to duty, so God calls to duty soldiers of all kinds and from every walk of life.

When we are called to duty as Christians, we are not perfect, (2 Timothy 1:7–10). We are like everyone else on journeys through this life. Perfection is not required for soldiers to go to war in a literal sense; neither is perfection required when a soldier of Christ goes to war in a spiritual sense.

Even though we are soldiers of the cross, we still make mistakes and fall down in our Christian duties. But unless we make mistakes and fall short of the glory of God, we cannot grow toward perfection, for perfection is a growth process, not something we are born possessing. Sage reminded herself that the Bible tells us that Christ is the only perfect being that has ever been born into this world and the only perfect being that will ever be born into this world. According to 2 Corinthians 5:21, Jesus was without sin; He knew no sin.

Sage realized that a person professing Christianity goes through a growth process on the way to perfection. A new Christian is a novice. Like babies, they require the sincere milk of the Word. Babies cannot eat or digest meat. Their bodies are not mature enough; they do not have the teeth or digestive system that can handle meat instead of milk.

Sage knew she had to become a baby first before she could become a mature Christian. Perfection was not her first stop on the journey.

> *2 Timothy 1:7–10: For God hath not given us the spirit of fear; but of power, and of love, and of sound mind. Be not thou therefore ashamed of the testimony of our Lord, nor of me his prisoner: but be thou partaker of the affliction of the gospel; according to the power of God. Who hath saved us, and called us with a holy calling, not according to our works, but according to his own purpose and grace, which was given in Christ Jesus before the world began. But, is now made manifest by the appearing of our Savior Jesus Christ, who hath abolished death and hath brought life and immortality to light through the gospel*

Perfection, for Sage, was the road less traveled as expressed by Robert Frost:

The Road Not Taken

> Two roads diverged in a yellow wood,
> And sorry I could not travel both
> And be one traveller, long I stood
> And looked down one as far as I could
> To where it bent in the undergrowth;
> Then took the other, as just as fair,
> And having perhaps the better claim,

Because it was grassy and wanted wear;
Though as far that the passing there
Had worn them really about the same,

And both that morning equally lay
In leaves no step had trodden black.
Oh, I kept the first for another day!
Yet knowing how way leads on to way,
I doubted if I should ever come back.

I shall be telling this with a sigh
Somewhere ages and ages hence:
Two roads diverged in a wood, and I—
I took the one less traveled by
And that has made all the difference …

    Sage considered what Frost said about "keeping the road for another day." She had gone down the wrong road for another day (two year's distance from God). As she considered that phrase, she doubted she would ever come back. But she finally realized that those two roads that diverged in a wood, whether equally worn or not, would lead her to the same place—back to God. All roads in life lead back to God.

    She did travel on the road that seemed to be the most used, but her journey would lead her back to the road that was less worn. The Bible tells us that wide is the way that leads to destruction (that road with leaves worn black with wear), and narrow is the way that leads to life, and there be few that find it (that road was grassy and wanted wear). "Enter ye in the straight gate; for wide is the gate, and broad is the way that leadeth to destruction, and many there be which go thereat" (Matt. 7:13).

    On the journey down the road which diverged in the wood so long ago, Sage knew she had taken the road most traveled, the one the Scripture calls the broad way. As with any road with which a traveler is not familiar, it was difficult to travel this broad road, and the directions were not easy to understand. A road that has so many different paths to it can get confusing to a traveler. The broad road offers so many different opportunities. These opportunities are traps. Sin is always a trap. The broad way might seem attractive and safe, but danger lurks on every side.

Some travelers' journeys take them the long way home. In contrast, other travelers' journeys take them the short way (the narrow road). Living in the world is like living in a circle. No matter at what point the journey starts, it ends up at the same place—back at the beginning. Sage knew her life was like living in a circle; she started with God, and she would end with God. This is a glaring reality, there for all to see. The Scripture tells us that in the beginning, God created the heaven and the Earth (Gen. 1:1). Sage knew that neither she nor anyone one else could get around this fact, no matter how hard they might try. He is the beginning and the end for everything and everyone.

Sage compared and contrasted perfection with a rose. A rose grows in beauty under the care of Mother Nature, but a rose has to be pruned in order for it to grow to its full beauty. In contrast, the beauty of an unpruned rose will not last, and the rose will die from the lack of care.

Sage, like the rose, knew she would need pruning by Jesus (Scripture) in order to grow to maturity to be the soldier Christ needs to fight this spiritual warfare. Sage, like soldiers in man's army (we call him Uncle Sam) and compared it to what armor the Scripture tells us we need to fight the spiritual warfare in Christ's army.

Ephesians 5:10–18 tells us to put on the whole armor of God: put on the helmet of salvation (soldiers wear helmets to protect their heads); the breastplate of righteousness (soldiers wear breastplates to protect their hearts and other vital organs); grid your loins about with truth (soldiers have ammunition belts and grenades to use to fight); shod your feet with the preparation of the Gospel of Peace (soldiers have soundly made boots for the walk that is necessary in their battle for peace).

> *Ephesians 5:10–18: Finally, my brethren, be strong in the Lord, and in the power of his might. Put on the whole armour of God that ye may be able to stand against the wiles of the devil. For we wrestle not against flesh and blood, nut against principalities, again powers, against the rulers of the darkness of this world, against spiritual wickedness in high places. Wherefore take unto you the*

whole armour of God that you might be able to stand in the evil day, and having done all, to stand. Stand therefore, having your lions girt with truth, and having on the breastplate of righteousness. And your feet shod with the preparation of the gospel of peace; Above all, taking the shield of faith, wherewith ye shall be able to quench all the fiery darts of the wicked. And take the helmet of salvation, and the sword of the spirit, which is the word of God; praying always with all prayer and supplication in the spirit, and watching thereunto with all perseverance and supplication for all saints.

Perfection is no pot of gold at the end of the rainbow; it is a growth process that all Christians go through during their entire journey on the way to eternity. Eternity is when we receive our crown of perfection. While we are here on Earth, we can be perfect in heart and mind by trying to do the will of God.

We can have the mind of Christ (I do all things to please my Father). We can also make sure everything we do in life is to please our God. We do not intentionally sin or fall short of the glory of God, but human flesh is not perfect. Sage also remembered what the Scripture said about how the body was formed; it came from dust and will go back to dust (Gen. 2:7).

Sage recalled what the apostle Paul said in Romans 7:14–25: sin in the physical body and the war that it rages with the inward man or spirit. We often do things or act in ways that are contrary to God's will or even our own true natures. Sage knew that her actions were not her true nature; rather they were born from the pain she experienced with the loss of her mother and sister.

In Romans chapter 6, Paul encourages or exhorts us not to let sin reign in our mortal bodies so that we obey its evil desires. Sage realized that this was a perfect description of her actions. There was a war going on between flesh and spirit. She had allowed herself to enter into a marriage with the world and left her first love, Jesus Christ (Elwell 2008, 939). Would she or could she find her way back?

According to Walter Elwell in *Baker Commentary on the Bible*, Paul views the believer as persona viator, a "person on the way." In this sense, he underscores the existential as well as the essential nature, the becoming as well as the being, of the Christian pilgrimage. The believer already has a new nature in Christ, but he must express this nature in Christ through decisive acts of choice and perseverance in faithfulness that confirm the fact, while the old nature lingers and must be daily repudiated as it wastes away (2008, 938).

> *Genesis 2:7: And the Lord God formed man of the dust of the ground, and breathed into his nostrils the breath of life; and man became a living soul.*

> *Romans 7:14–25: For we know that the law is spiritual; but I am carnal, sold under sin. For that which I do I allow not: For what I would, that do I not: but what I hate, that do I. If then I do that which I would not, I consent unto the law that is good. Now, them it is no more I that do it, but sin that dwelleth in me. For I know that in me (that is in my flesh,) dwelleth no good thing: for to will is present with me: but how to perform that which is good I find not. For the good that I would not: but the evil which I would not that I do. Now, if I do that which I would not, it is no more I that do it, but that sin dwelleth in me. I find then a law, that, when I would do good evil is present with me. For I delight in the law of God after the inward man. But, I see another law in my members, and bringing me into captivity to the law of sin which is in my members. O wretched man that I am! Who shall deliver me from the body of this death? I thank God through Jesus Christ our Lord. So than with the mind I serve the law of God; but with the flesh the law of sin.*

What a change had taken place in Sage by this point in her life; it was difficult for her to come to the realization that life and God were not how she perceived them. Sage had her own recipe for what salvation was and who God was, and she had refused to see the truth the Scripture gives us about who God is, what salvation is, and how we must live our lives.

Sage's mind went back to making a cake or any other food items from a recipe. She could change any part of a man-made recipe that she wanted. Ingredients can be added to a recipe or taken away and or changed to fit a particular taste. The *big* change Sage had to accept was that she could not change the recipe God has written for man. We cannot add to or take away from the truth about God to fit our lives or particular situations. Without the ingredients that God has put into the recipe for man's life, we would not be pleasing to God.

Sage had always wanted to take out a step in the recipe process to make it fit her situation. She thought about the Sunday mornings when she was growing up. Her mom would get her up at 6:00 AM to make the cake for the family dinner. This irritated Sage because she had two other sisters that could bake a cake, but Mom only wanted her to make it.

Sage would put the cake together like she wanted it, not like the box said. Surprisingly, the cakes always came out beautifully.

"This is why," Sage's mother told her, "I want you to make the cakes. I just never know what surprise I will get each Sunday morning, and it is a joy to me to see you be so creative and use that unlimited imagination of yours."

God does not operate in that manner. We cannot change the prescription of life, and we cannot decide when and how God is supposed to help. In essence, we cannot dictate to God. Sage had to face this reality. The Scripture tells us that God said, "I am the Lord Thy God and I change not" (Mal. 3:6).

Sage realized life is not about living forever here on Earth but making the journey here on Earth count. The Scripture tells us that we are on a journey; we sojourn in this land on our way to our eternal home. Just as our physical bodies have houses to live in, so do our spiritual beings; they are housed within our bodies, their homes (1 Cor. 6:19). Our physical bodies die slowly on our journey through life. It is like pulling off a garment. Each year we live, we leave some of our youth and one more yesterday behind.

Sage began to realize that lilies die and are reborn every season. Dysantha's season had come, and she died and would be reborn as an eternal soul solely in God's hands—a just God who created this beautiful creature (her sister). And as the Scripture expresses clearly, we are born from dust and will return to dust (Gen. 2:7).

> *I Corinthians 6:19: What? Know ye not that your body is the temple of the Holy Ghost which is in you, which ye have of God, and ye are not your own.*

The Scripture tells us that God only promises us a journey of three score and ten years and eighty years by reason of strength (Ps. 90:10), but He did not promise us how many of the three score and ten years we would live. Sage realized that her sister Dysantha had lived her three score and ten years according to God's count, not man's.

She also realized that death, too, is a change. She compared death to going through a door. Once that door is closed, there is no key to open it; it is a door with a lock on one side only—God's side, not man's. Sage knew that her sister's death was another stop on her journey to eternity—the last stop.

Dysantha's pain and suffering was a change Sage could not accept. To know and see her sister in unbearable pain from chemotherapy and radiation was like a death in and of itself. No one should have to suffer through such agony. Sage's attitude about her sister began to change. Life had taught her a hard lesson.

Sage had lived in a dark valley for too long without the light. She seemed to stumble in the darkness for more than two years. Grasping for straws of understanding had not gotten her very far. Sage felt like the Bible's description of the children of Israel wandering in the desert for forty years without anything about them changing (Deut. 29:5–6). Their wandering in the desert for forty years was a cleansing process. The cleansing process finally brought them to the Jordan River.

Sage, like the children of Israel, after wandering in a dark valley for more than two years, had come to her Jordon River. The children of Israel, according to Joshua 5:6 crossed into the promised land flowing with milk and honey. Crossing her Jordan River into her land of milk and honey would be a change for Sage. She would have to come back to God and hear His voice once again. The Lord's church is man's land of milk and honey in this century, his kingdom. Milk and honey represent the best; it says prosperity (Matt. 16:18).

Sage had been away from God for so long, what would she say? What reason could she offer for blaming Him for her sister's death? How could she ask for forgiveness for her leaving the security God provides while we are in His hands, turning her back to God, and looking to the world for comfort after Dysantha's death?

This would be another hard change for Sage to make and face. Sage knew she had egregiously overstepped the bounds with God. God seeketh those to serve Him in spirit and in truth (John 4:23–24). Like Adam and Eve, Sage's sin had convicted her because of her disobedience (Gen. 3:8–10).

> *Psalms 90:10: The days of our years are three-score years and ten; and if by reason of strength they be fourscore years, yet is their strength labour and sorrow; for it is soon cut off, and we fly away.*

> *Deuteronomy 29:5–6: And I have led you forty years in the wilderness: your clothes are not waxen upon you, and thy shoe is not waxen old upon thy foot. Ye have not eaten bread, neither have ye drunk wine or strong drink: that ye might know that I am the Lord your God.*

> *Joshua 5:6: For the children of Israel walked forty years in the wilderness, till all the people that were men of war; which came out of Egypt, were consumed, because they obeyed not the voice of the Lord: unto whom the Lord sware to their fathers that he would give us, a land that floweth with milk and honey.*

Matthew 16:18: And I say unto thee, that thou art Peter, and upon this rock I will build my church; and the gates of hell shall not prevail against it.

John 4:23–24: The Father seeketh those who will worship him. God is a spirit and they that worship him must worship him in spirit and in truth.

Genesis 3:8–10: Ibid.

Chapter 11

The Mountain

The word of God to Sage was like the lake that stands at Northwest Trek in Washington State (Northwest Trek 2006). Sage visited her brother Josef in 2006, and the Northwest Trek Wildlife Park was one of the sights she visited.

In reflection, Sage compared the beauty of the Word of God to that fifty-thousand-year-old lake that welcomes visitors as they enter the preservation area. The lake's waves rippled softly along the shore, and the water glistened and danced in the sun like crystal dishes set for an elaborate dinner. The lake stood firm and strong, with an unchanging and timeless beauty, so like the Word of God—timeless, beautiful, and unchanging.

Sage also visited Mount Rainier. She compared God to Mount Rainier—strong, timeless, and beautiful. Like God, the mountain never changes; only the conditions or situations around it alter. Sage thought back and looked at her life … God had never changed as Sage had presupposed early on in her journey. The situation and events surrounding her life were what changed. God, like the mountain, had not moved.

So it brought Sage to the conclusion that a walk with God demands that she move toward the mountain and not expect the mountain to move toward her. The Scripture tells us, "Pride goeth before destruction and a haughty spirit before a fall" (Prov. 16:18). Sage had taken a fall. She had nowhere to go now. She had come face-to-face with the truth: God had come as close as He was going to; it was up to Sage to move the rest of the way.

Life at the foot of Mount Rainier, she noticed, was rich and luscious; flowers bloomed even in the freezing cold weather. Sage knew her life would thrive at the foot of the mountain also. Like the flowers and greenery, which relied on the mountain for survival, she would have to rely on God for everything for her spiritual and physical survival.

The Scripture tells us in Jeremiah 10:23–24, "It is not in man to direct his footsteps, but is directed by every word that proceedeth out of the mouth of God." Sage knew she had to depend on God. She could not travel this hard road alone. There were too many traps and dangers that existed without the help of God. Sage had tried to direct her own path for many years, but she had gotten nowhere, made no progress, and had found no peace.

> *Proverbs 16: 17–18: The highway of the upright is to depart from evil: he that keepeth his way preserveth his soul. Pride goeth before destruction and a haughty spirit before a fall.*
>
> *Jeremiah 10:23–24: O Lord, I know that the way of man is not in himself; it is not in man that walketh to direct his steps. O Lord, correct me, but with judgment; not in thine anger, lest thou bring me to nothing.*

God's word is like the melting snow in early spring. The water replenishes the Earth. Like the greenery and flowers, which waited patiently for the renewing effect of the water, man must also rely on the renewing effect that comes from God's grace and mercy.

The limbs of a tree are lifeless if they are not attached to the trunk; so is the life of a man who is not attached to God. Under the shadow of the Almighty, as the greenery and plants under the shadow of the mountain, we get all that is necessary for life and survival.

Chapter 12

Joy Comes in the Morning

During her journey in the world, Sage felt that she had been in perils of distress and the deep and had received her forty stripes less one. She compared what she felt and encountered to what Paul said he suffered from the world in 2 Corinthians 11:25–26:

Thrice was I beaten with rods, once was I stoned, thrice I suffered shipwreck, a night and a day I have been in the deep; In journeying often, in perils of waters, in perils of robbers, in perils of mine own countrymen, in perils by the heathen, in perils in the city, in perils in the wilderness, in perils in the sea, in perils among false brethren; In weariness and painfulness, in watching's often, in hunger and thirst, in fasting often, in cold and nakedness.

All of these things Sage had suffered while in the world. It was not the kind place she thought it was going to be. She had suffered these things spiritually, emotionally, socially, and physically.

Sage knew that the light affliction, which is but for a moment, worketh for us. It is a far more exceeding and eternal weight of glory. Dysantha and Maria had light affliction compared to our Lord and Savior Jesus Christ, as we all have here on this Earth. According to 2 Corinthians 4:18, no suffering here on Earth can compare to the glory that we will receive in eternity. Sage searched the depths of her spirit to see if she would be worthy of this exceeding and eternal weight of glory.

The light of heaven shined through, and the shadows of Earth faded. Crying does endure for a night, but joy comes in the morning, (Ps. 30:5).

Sage had found joy and peace again in Jesus Christ, her Lord and Savior, after many years of pain and agony. She no longer wandered lost in the world because she was no more of the world, but rather she lived in the world and was of God's Kingdom once again.

Sage had been reborn again through Christ Jesus, into His grace and mercy. Her unresolved pain and glaring inability to deal with her mother and sister's deaths were gone. She knew she would always miss her loved ones, but she could face their deaths now with a mature understanding of life and death; they go together and cannot be separated.

Sage was now singing a new song—a song of joy, peace, and happiness, (Isa. 42:10–11). Even though other trials on the journey home would beset her and her family, she now had a new footing, a firmer foundation. She did not feel hopelessness anymore; in its place, she felt hope. Before, her life had been built on shifting sands that moved constantly, but now she stood on solid rock, and that rock was Christ.

> *Psalms 30:5: For his anger endureth but a moment: in his favor is life: weeping may endure for a night, but joy comes in the morning*

> *Isaiah 42:10–11: Sing unto the Lord a new song and his praise from the end of the earth, ye that go down to the sea, and all that is therein; the isles, and the inhabitants*

thereof. Let the wilderness and the cities thereof lift up their voice, the villages that Kedar doth inhabit: let the inhabitants of the rock sing, let them shout from the top of the mountains.

Luke 6:47–49 tells us that building on sand is sure destruction. When storms come and rains of life set in, the sands will not hold. Sand soaks up a lot of water, but it cannot hold that water, and in the end the sands are washed away. But if you build your hope upon the solid rock, even though waters of life wash across the rock, they slide right off; the waters do not soak in as they do in sand. Jesus is the solid rock that our hope must be built upon; He can withstand all the storms and rains life can throw at us if we dwell under the shadow of the Almighty.

Being apathetic or lethargic is deadly spiritually. Man cannot afford a lackluster attitude. We cannot display before God or to God an uninterested attitude toward His commandments and His will for our lives. This distance from God was just as painful to Sage as her mother's and sister's deaths. Sage had to repent before she could be joyful again, but her repentance would be a joy to the Father and the angels of heaven (Luke 15:10).

Luke 6:47–49: Whosoever cometh to me, and heareth my sayings, and doeth them, I will shew you to whom he is like: He is like a man which built an house, and digged deep, and laid the foundation on a rock: and when the flood arose, the stream beat vehemently upon that house, and could not shake it: for it was founded upon a rock. But, he that heareth, and doeth not, is like a man that without a foundation built an house upon the earth; against which the stream did beat vehemently, and immediately it fell; and the ruin of that house was great.

Luke 15:10: Angels rejoiced one sinner that repents.

Chapter 13

The Clouds Are Gone

We are not in step with God. Rather, we are walking in His footsteps, for God is the leader, the light on our pathway. A journey in darkness requires light. Man cannot provide light; only God can. His word is a lamp unto our feet and a light upon our pathway (Ps. 109:115).

The pathway is a narrow one; we search for God with our hearts, not our eyes. Our physical light helps us find our way in the physical world in which we live. Sage thought that on a journey, man made many stops in life; our physical eyes help us see in order to live in this physical world. She realized she would have to use spiritual sight in the search for God. She would have to look for God with her heart and not her eye.

Clouds had covered Sage for many years, keeping her in darkness, which causes all of us to go astray: "He that walketh in darkness knoweth not where he is going" (John 12:35b). Man's physical eye is not programmed to see in darkness without the proper light. For man, the eye is the light in the mind but not in darkness.

Clouds cover light; they create a hazy or dim view. The death of Maria and Dysantha formed a dark cloud over Sage. Sage realized God does not make mistakes. Neither is He cruel or unkind. Instead He is loving, gentle, caring, and protective of His children. Sage constantly reminded herself of what the psalmist tells us in Psalm 30:5; 30: 11–12: "Crying endureth for a night; but, joy comes in the morning…Thou hast turned for me my mourning into dancing; thou hast put off my sackcloth, and girded me with gladness; to the end that my glory may sing praise unto thee, and not be silent. O Lord my God, I will give thanks unto thee forever."

God can turn your mourning into dancing, take away the burden (that sackcloth), gird you with a new garment (gladness), and turn away His intended punishment for disobedience. Wearing sackcloth is not a pleasant task; it is a burden. There is no beauty in sackcloth, for sackcloth covers beauty. Sackcloth was fashioned from camel or goat hair to be worn as a sign of anguish or mourning. According to Isaiah 58:5b–6, "…a day for a man to afflict his soul? Is it to bow down his head as a bulrush and spread sackcloth and ashes over him. I have chosen this fast to loosen the bands of wickedness, to undo the heavy burdens, and let the oppressed to, and that ye break every yoke."

When preaching to the citizens of Nineveh to avert the pending doom that God had intended for that city, this was the king's command: "But let everyman be covered with sackcloth, and cry mightily unto God; yea, let them turn everyone from his evil way, and from the violence that is in his hands, who can tell if God will turn and repent and turn away from the fierce anger, that we perish not," (Jon. 3:8–9). Sage prayed that God would forgive her for losing her way and going into the world for comfort: Thy word is a lamp unto my feet and a light unto my pathway (Ps. 119:105).

Ephesians 4:23–24 tell us, "And be renewed in the spirit of your mind; and that ye put on the new man made after righteousness and true holiness." We must put off the old man and put on the new that is created in true holiness. Sage had not displayed this in her character as a Christian. We must leave behind the burden that once weighed us down. Trials and tribulations are of the world, not of God. But He can move them for you. The psalmist said that he turned for me, my mourning into dancing—into gladness. Sage said that she felt the yoke of sin had been broken and God had turned his anger away from God.

Spiritual sight is far more beneficial than physical sight. If Sage had been looking at the tragedy that occurred with her sister and mother with a spiritual eye, she would not have gotten so far off track and taken the wrong path. Playing a blame game with God does not benefit mankind in any way. We blame and accuse and become angry, disillusioned, and untrusting of God. God is not the cause of the evil diseases that ravish our love ones' bodies and take their lives.

Evil and sickness exist because this world is not a perfect place. We are on a journey through this world to a perfect place where there is no sickness, sadness, or disease—only peace and a future with God, who will give us an immoral body, free of any worldly element.

The clouds were gone, and Sage was seeing clearly again, looking with a spiritual eye and not a physical eye. Sage remembered what the Scripture said about worshiping God: "The father seeth those who will worship him. God is a spirit and they that worship Him must worship Him in spirit and in truth" (John 4:23–24).

Sage was singing a new song, ascribing to God honor and glory. "Give unto God the glory due unto his name; worship the Lord in the beauty of his holiness" (Ps. 29:2). That beauty is beyond description; there is no unrighteousness in God, only beauty, love, splendor, and magnificence. He is a God of pleasing and impressive characteristics. There are no flaws in God.

A.W. Tozer said, "God did not write a book and send it by messenger to be read at a distance by unaided minds. He spoke a book and lives in his spoken words, constantly speaking his words and causing the power of them to persist across the years" (2001).

Sage had to empty herself of the world and all that it held to her as peace and safety. It was a scary thought to leave what had become safety for her way back to Christ. The road was hard; it was the same on the trip back as it had been on the trip going away from God.

Heartache, pain, agony, aloneness, fear, rage, disbelief, confusion—all of these emotions do not describe a relationship with Jesus but truly with the world. God does not reject His children, but He welcomes them with open arms. He always gives His children the best. Sage had become a child again before God, with no will of her own, innocent before God, looking to Him for forgiveness and help—help she could not find in the world. Like the Prodigal Son, the world and what it has to offer only brings starvation, loneliness, fear, and destitution of the spirit.

Only God can cure these ills in man. He is always willing, if we will only come to Him. The Prodigal Son had to let go of His pride and go home. Christ tells us this in Matthew 11:28–30: "Come to me all ye that labor and are heavy laden and I will give you rest. Take my yoke and learn of me and find peace for your soul."

The Prodigal Son left the safety of His Father's home for what He thought was a better place—the world. Sage, like the Prodigal Son, left her Father in heaven because of the pain and suffering she experienced in the loss of her mother and sister. She thought the world would be her friend, as did the Prodigal Son, but increased heartache, trouble, destitution, and starvation beset the Prodigal Son physically. These were the same symptoms that beset Sage spiritually.

The Prodigal Son had to resort to eating the same food designed for pigs. He encountered rejection after all His physical riches were gone. Sage had also encountered rejection after her spiritual riches were gone. The world in and of itself does not hold any peace, joy, help, or comfort when you are in need; total rejection will be your experience, as it was for Sage and the Prodigal Son. Sometimes we then have big mental bubbles that we create around ourselves, or we fly our big mental balloons, thinking there is something better out there in the world. All too soon we find out how wrong we are. We walk around in our bubbles, flying our balloons of pride as if we have blinders on. We are in fact spiritually blind and destitute from God's care. The Bible demonstrates this plainly through Jesus's parable and story of the Prodigal Son:

> And not many days after the younger son gather all together, and took his journey into a far country, and there wasted his substance with riotous living. And when he had spent all, there arose a mighty famine in that land; and he began to be in want. And he went and joined himself to a citizen of that country; and he sent him into his fields to feed swine. And he would fain have filled his belly with the husks that the swine did eat: and no man gave unto him.

And when he came to himself, he said, How many hired servants of my father's have bread enough and to spare, and I perish with hunger. I will arise and go to my father, and will say to him, Father; I have sinned against heaven and before thee. And am no more worthy to be called the son: make me as one of they hired servants. And he arose, and came to his father. But when he was yet a great way off, his father saw him, and had compassion, and ran, and fell on his neck, and kissed him. And the son said unto him, Father, I have sinned against heaven, and in thy sight, and am not more worthy to be called thy son. But the father said to the servants, Bring forth the best robe, and put it on him; and put a ring on his hand, and shoes on his feet: And bring hither the fatted calf, and kill it; and let us eat, and be merry; for my son was dead, and is alive again, he was lost and is found. And they began to be merry. It is meet that we should make merry, and be glad: for this thy brother was dead, and is alive again: and was lost, and is found. (Luke 15:11–31)

Sage told me that the song, "On Bended Knees I Come" comes to mind when she thinks of the story of the Prodigal Son's return to His Father's house, just as He returned to her Father's house: "On bended knee I come/with a broken heart I come/bowing down before your holy throne/As I look upon your face/show your mercy and your grace/Change my life O Holy Spirit/make me fresh and ever new/Make my life a holy sacrifice to you" (Gay, 1988).

God counsels us in Revelations 3:18, "To buy from me gold tried in the fire, that thou mayest be rich; and white raiment, that thou mayest cover your shameful nakedness; and salve to put on your eyes, so you can see." We cannot buy this from the world; there is a *no sale or sold out* sign up everywhere you turn. The world poses too many hurdles to jump. The hurdles got too high for Sage and the Prodigal Son. In this context, Jesus demands we do three things; all must be done to be successful and pleasing to God: 1) buy; 2) gold; 3) tried by fire. It withstands the test of time; you cannot get this type of gold anywhere else, certainly not the world. This foundation can no other man lay than the one laid by Jesus Christ (1 Cor. 3:11–15).

> *1 Corinthians 3:11–15: For no one can lay any foundation other than the one already laid, which is Jesus Christ. If anyone builds on this foundation using gold, silver, costly stones, wood, hay or straw their work will be shown for what it is, because the day will bring it to light. It will he revealed with fire, and the fire will test the quality of each person's work. If what has been built survives, the builder will receive a reward. If it is burned up, the builder will suffer loss but yet will be saved even though only as one escaping through the flames.*

Building your hopes or putting trust in wood, hay, and stubble will fail; these are perishable things. The world cannot offer you gold that is tried by fire. The only gold the world can provide melts when the fire gets too hot. Gold purchased from Jesus is lasting; it has withstood the test of time.

Jesus paid the price on the cross for us to stand before God with acceptable works, to be able to wear the white raiment that stands for purity, and to have spiritual eyes that can see (when we look with worldly eyes, we are blind to what God would have us to do) that has been anointed with the salve of spirituality, the Word of God.

Sage suffered as much after she found her way again as she had when she first lost her way. She felt remorse and regret for blaming God because she lost her loved ones. Losing a loved one is painful, but losing two loved ones is more than the mind can comprehend, especially if those loved ones are as close as a dear, precious mother and a beloved sister.

A heavy, contrite heart was how Sage described her feelings about her actions toward her heavenly Father. But a journey can be a teacher as well as an eye-opener in life. A journey can give us a new direction. Not direction in this sense of north, south, east, or west, but rather direction in a way of thinking, a change in mindset that gives the journeyman a new focus, a focus of being realistic.

A contrite heart is a sorrowful heart; Jesus said those with a sorrowful heart are blessed (Matt. 5:4): Blessed are those that mourn for they shall be comforted. A contrite heart should be one that questions motives and actions without using any reasonability or sensibility when facing tragedy of death. God did not promise us a perfect life, void of trouble, heartache, or pain. Most certainly our Lord and Savior did not live this type of life when He was here on Earth. But rather, He learned obedience by the things He suffered (Heb. 5:8).

In this light, we too, as instructed by the Lord, are to pick up our crosses and follow Him. He never promised that our crosses, whatever they might be, were going to be easy, pleasant, tasteful, or painless. There is no growth where there is no suffering. The things we suffer on our spiritual journeys, like our physical journeys, have hidden trouble, pain, heartache, and setbacks. All of these are modeled through life.

But our spiritual journeys—with their heartaches, pain, and suffering—bring us to a journey's end that has joy, peace, and eternal salvation for our souls, thereby giving us the right to live forever with God and our Lord and Savior Jesus Christ. Our spiritual journeys should stand up to the test, be tried by fire, and emerge on the other side of trouble, heartache, and loss of a loved one stronger and more resilient.

This warfare we fight within us or outside us is a battle to the end—we win, or we lose. Winning entitles us to eternity; losing will send us to eternal damnation. Sage realized that blindness and irrational thinking about God is a trick of the devil. He uses whatever wiles he can and catches humans at their weakest moments, like a thief in the night. John 10:1–5 tells us that a thief or robber climbs up some other way, as does Satan. Satan does not engage his adversary in frontal attacks any more than a thief does. The thief, like Satan, comes when you least expect it and at inopportune times.

At the foot of the mountain, there is luscious greenery that has benefited from the love, care, and food that flows from the throne of God, our Father. The mountain, that solid rock, does not move or change. He is that solid rock we can depend on. There are no *no sale* or *sold out* signs ever posted in God's Kingdom. We always have the opportunity and chance to come home. He constantly looks for His lost sheep (Luke 15:4–7). For the Bible tells us plainly: "He came to seek and save the lost. For it is not his will that any should perish" (Matt. 18:12–14). "We go astray like sheep, but are now returned unto Christ the Shepherd and Bishop of our souls" (1 Peter 2:25). A bishop is an inspector (he certifies us), a watchman looks after us to make sure we do not go astray (he guards against the adversary, Satan), the overseer has the authority to do what is necessary to make sure his sheep are successful in the salvation provided (he spiritually feeds the flock). God never gives up on us; we are the ones who give up on God, as well as ourselves. Satan loves quitters. In fact, he bets on us quitting. He did on Job (Job 1:8–15). But Satan lost his bet with God. Job did not turn; instead he stayed strong in his resolve and faith.

> *John 10:1-5: Verily, verily, I say unto you, He that entereth not by the door into the sheepfold, but climeth up some other way, the same is a thief and a robber. But he that entereth in by the door is the shepherd of the sheep. To him the porter openeth; and the sheep hear his voice: and he calleth his own sheep by name, and leadeth them out. And when he putteth forth his own sheep, he goeth before them, and the sheep follow him: for they know his voice. And a stranger will they not follow, but will flee with him: for they know not the voice of strangers.*
>
> *Hebrews 5:8 Ibid*
>
> *Job 1:8–11: And the Lord said unto Satan, hast thou considered my servant Job, that there is none like him on earth, a perfect and upright man, and one that feareth God, and escheweth evil? The Satan answered the Lord, and said, doth Job fear God for nought? Hast not thou made a hedge around him, and about his house, and*

about all that he hath on every side? Thou hast blessed the work of his hands, and his substance is increased in the land. But put forth thine hand now, and touch all that he hath, and he will curse thee to thou face.

Luke 15:4–7: What man of you, have an hundred sheep if he lose one of them, doth not leave the ninety and nine in the wilderness and go after that which is lost, until he find it? And when he has found it, he layeth it on his shoulder, rejoicing, and when he cometh home, he calleth together his friends and neighbors, saying unto them, rejoice with me for I have found my sheep which was lost; I say to you; that likewise joy shall be in heaven over one sinner that repenteth, more than over ninety and nine just persons, which need no repentance.

Chapter 14

The Finished Life

Sage considered her mother one of the wisest people in the world. According to Sage, "A girl's mother is always wise because she has seen and experienced lots of life and has gone through many changes that have left scars of wisdom on her heart and mind." Listening to other females talk about their mothers, Sage often wondered why they were not more appreciative of their mothers and the experiences and knowledge they had gained in their lifetime?

Sage remembered her mother telling her that daughters, young women especially, think they know everything. They see their mothers as old and outdated and don't think they know what is "hip" and what is "now." But as we look down life's road, we become our mothers, whether we want to or not. Wise or unwise, we are them. We grow older and raise children that become the way we were as children, thinking their parents are outdated and not "hip." And so the cycle goes on.

The many wise words Maria shared with her children were etched in Sage's memory. Life is a very wise teacher to those who desire to learn.

Sage was glad for her mother's wisdom. She did not consider her mother outdated or unhip. Recalling some of her mother's wisdom helped Sage get through the difficult times. She faced all that tragedy in her life by leaning on that wisdom. But time and the bell tolls for each of us; it had tolled for her mother and sister. She could no longer lean upon this wisdom. Maria died in October 1977; therefore, Sage had to invoke her memory.

So, young women (and even young men), be thankful and appreciative of your mothers, for they are wise and have lived the lessons they share with you. At the end of our journeys, our mothers' wisdom has already been there. Cherish your mother and that relationship so that it becomes part of you.

When your mother is gone, the world takes on a different look. It is not the same joyful place it was when your mom was in your life. Mothers are untapped treasure with which we are blessed. They are one of God's greatest gifts. Each one is lovingly unique. Mothers spell love and sacrifice (Prov. 31).

> *Proverbs 31: Who can find a virtuous woman? For her price is far above rubies. The heart of her husband doth safely trust in her, so the he shall have no need of spoil. She will do him good and not evil all the day of her life. She seeketh wool, and flax, and worketh willingly with her hands. She is like the merchants' ships; she bringeth her food from afar. She riseth also while it is yet night, and giveth meat to her household; and a portion to her maidens. She considereth a field, and buyeth it: with the fruit of her hands she planet a vineyard. She girdeth her lions with strength and strengthened her arms. She preceiveth the merchandise is good; her candle goeth not out by night. She layeth her hands to the spindle, and hands hold the distaff. She stretcheth out her hand to the poor, yea; she reacheth forth her hands to the needy. She is not afraid of the snow for her household: for all her household are clothed with scarlet. She maketh herself covering of tapestry; her clothing is like silk and purple. Her husband is known in the gate, when he sitteth among the elders of the land. She maketh fine linen, and selleth*

it: and delivereth girdles unto the merchant. Strength and honor are her clothing: and she shall rejoice in time to come. She openeth her mouth with wisdom: and in her tongue is the law of kindness. She looketh well to the ways of her household; and eateth not the bread of idleness. Her children arise up, and call her blessed: her husband also, and he praiseth her. Many daughters have done virtuously, but thou excellest them all. Favour is deceitful, and beauty is vain: but a woman that feareth the Lord, she shall be praised. Give her the fruit of her hands; and let her own works praise her in the gates.

Mothers are

- the strength in the family;
- the glue that holds the family together;
- the ones who make the house a home;
- someone who can make any problem disappear;
- one way to spell *love*; and
- a blessing from God.

Hold tight to these precious jewels, because when they are gone, your world will change. When you lose a mother, you lose a lot. Jewels are precious stones, desirable because of their rareness, hardness, and beauty (The Master Study Bible, King James Version 2001, B-443). Maria was precious, rare, sturdy, and beautiful. Beauty does not necessarily mean physical beauty, which she had, but rather it means that beauty shined through from the inside to give her a beautiful glow.

Sisters are best friends, strong trees that do not break in a storm but rather sway with the wind. This was the description Sage gave of her sister Dysantha.

I asked Sage what would Dysantha tell her now?

Sage said if her sister Dysantha could talk to her now, she would tell Sage, "As a rose fades, so will you. Rose petals fall away and wither with time. Life is like a rose petal: it withers little by little. Some roses last longer or have longer life spans than others. My life span (my petals) lasted their lifetime, as did my God-given days on Earth. My days may have seemed short to you, but they were not to me. I lived my dream on my journey home. I am at peace—no more pain, no more sorrow, just endless joy each day. So, pet, don't grieve for me anymore; you were a precious little sister to me, my baby. Your rose petals have not fallen or withered; live your life in joy and be at peace with my death. And when your rose petals wither and fall and your life fades like the evening sun in the western sky, when the sun sets and your life ends, I will be waiting for you."

Sage said, "My sister and mother did not leave unfinished lives; they both lived full lives. While we are here on this Earth, this is the road we need to take. Live a full life. A full life has nothing to do with age but rather what you've done with your God-given time while you were here."

Sage finally realized that all of the time she had thought she was away from God, she had been closer than ever, because during her grief and pain, He held her close to Him and carried her each step of the way. Sage saw clearly the footprints in the sand. were too large be hers; shocked she realized they were God's.

"Footprints in the Sand," a poem by Mary Stevenson had always meant a lot to Sage; she recalled her favorite verses of the poem:

> The Lord replied:
> My son, my precious child,
> I love you and I would never leave you.
> During the times of trials and suffering,
> When you see only one set of footprints,
> It was then I carried you.

Sage went from spiritual hopelessness to spiritual hope. Her search for God had led her to the same place she had been before tragedy engulfed her life. Sage realized that God does not leave His children when they are in dark places that cause them agony and grief, but He is always with His children. For He indeed says, "I will never leave thee nor forsake thee" (Deut. 31:8).

Sage knew her mother and sister would tell her the following about grieving for loved ones that are gone from this life as we know it:

Grieve Not for Me

I cannot let you grieve for me,
For those who love must let us go.
In comfort, please believe I'm free,
From all the pain life can bestow,

As I begin my world anew,
Consider not what used to be,
I'm sending happy smiles to you
While I enjoy eternity

Lord, bless the home, from which I came,
Yet, brush each lonely hour away,
With fond remembrance of my name,
And sunshine for a newer day.
Look to the wind to find me there
Besides the hardest thing you do.
I've left my love within this prayer.
I'm always watching over you. (Anonymous)

Deuteronomy 31:8: It is the Lord who goes before you. He will be with you; he will not leave your or forsake you. Do not be fear or be dismayed.

Chapter 15

Life's Lessons: A Mother's Wisdom

Sage had always been the "radical" one in her family, even as a child. She resisted change at all cost. She was not willing to change, and when she was, it was only under certain conditions. Change was almost situational for her; if the situation was not convenient or to her liking, she would refuse to be swayed one way or the other.

Being the "radical" one is why Sage had suffered at different points in her life. She remembered two incidents in particular when she did not do as her mother asked; she even stated her case, even though it was dangerous and could get her into the proverbial hot water with her mom. She sometimes challenged Maria, stating her sound reason for not obeying (smarting off at the mouth is what her mother called it).

Maria's response would be, "I will slap you into next week."

"That is a long way, Mama. I might not be able to get back," Sage would immediately retort.

"Sage, are you being smart?" Maria would then ask.

Sage usually said something like, "No, Mama, just making an observation; you wouldn't want to lose your baby daughter now would you?"

Sage recalled some of the things her mother told her as she grew and matured as a young adult. Looking back, Sage could see exactly what her mother meant during her childhood when it had been so hard for her see her mother's wisdom as being helpful in life.

Sage said she can take flight and return to her childhood, as Richard MacWilliams clearly points out in the poem "Free Spread the Wings of Mystery." The poem reads, "Free spread the wings of mystery,/Free spread to the hills and dales of my youth."

Sage shared some of the wise sayings her mother had taught her children. She was glad to have these quaint expressions of her mother's, which she had heard all of her life:

- Make peace with the past so it won't screw up the present.
- Don't compare your life to others'; you have no idea what their journeys are all about.
- God don't blink; He is ever-watchful.
- God loves you because of who God is, not because of something you did or didn't do.
- All that truly matters in the end is that you've loved.
- Be yourself and not an imitation of others or what others want you to be.
- Life's degree is obtained through the school of hard knocks.
- Don't worry. As long as people are talking about you, you are important; it's when they quit that you need to be worried.
- Don't stand outside a window and look at someone else's life; it does not compare with your own.
- Life is a wise teacher to those who desire to learn.
- Each human makes his or her own footprints. Success in life is not judged by the size of the footprint but by the size of the human and what legacy he or she leaves that can be passed on.

- Bitterness is an evil taskmaster.
- We cannot live in the past, the present, and the future all at once. The past is gone, we live in the present, and the future is ahead of us.
- Don't stand in the shadows of life. Stand in the light where you can see and be seen.
- Mediocre is not acceptable in the Seymour family; do your best at all time.
- *Can't* isn't a word that is used in this family; only *can* is acceptable.
- People don't want to see you every time they open their door; let them be glad you visited, not thinking *here she or he comes again!*
- Belief in self equals survival.
- Doubt is a recipe for failure.
- There are just as many short graves as there are long; not only older people die.
- It is not always the leaning tree that falls.

Sage Alyantha Seymour had grown to be a wise and very successful woman. She was confident, loving, kind, helpful, and—above all—a child of the King. Her journey was now clear to her; her footsteps were set on the right path. She was no longer angry but had accepted God's will for her life.

She now had peace in her soul. She thought of the verse of the song "It Is Well with My Soul." It goes, "When peace like a river attendeth my way/when sorrows like sea billow roll/whatever my lot/it has taught me to say/It is well/ it is well/with my soul."

Chapter 16

Conclusion: The New Man

Sage allowed herself to feel, to be angry, to hide in a dark place, and to be thankful for the light because it brings reality. The stages of death for Sage were disbelief, anger, hurt, total rejection, bewilderment, frightened, madness, and hate.

After two years of going down that wide way, she had finally found acceptance, resignation, understanding, and forgiveness of herself for not being able to help her sister or her mother, which had not been in her power anyway. Help and hope is of God our Father and our Lord and Savior Jesus Christ.

She had finally resigned herself to the fact that her sister and mother were gone and would not return. Even though the loss of a loved one is one of the most devastating feelings in the world, there was nothing she could have done for them. The grief she felt was normal. Her ability to help was hopeless (human) when it comes to illness and death.

Death is death, whether it is spiritual or physical; they both had the same results for Sage. Her mother and sister experienced a physical death, which is far less dangerous than the spiritual death Sage experienced. A spiritual death is separation from God. The physical death is separation from the physical world on your way home to God.

Sage was now dead to the physical world and alive to the spiritual world. In Roman 7:15 and 7:24, Paul said, "The things that I hate that I do, the things that I should do I do not, O' Wretched man that I am." Sage had finally found peace through the grace of God. She had a favorite song she sang when she thought of the matchless grace of God and His forgiving nature: "Grace Greater than Our Sin." I wish you could have heard her sing; she has a beautiful voice, this wonderful, hidden talent. The following is her favorite verse in the song: "Marvelous infinite, matchless grace, freely bestowed on all who believe/You that are longing to see his face//Will you this moment his grace receive?/Grace, grace, God's grace/Grace that will pardon and cleanse within;/Grace, grace God's grace/Grace that is greater than all our sin" (Johnson 1994, 110–111).

Ephesians 2:4–10 tells us, "But God, who is rich in mercy, for his great love wherewith he loved us. Even when we were dead in sins, hath quickened us together with Christ, (by grace ye are saved;) and hath raised us up together, and made us sit together in heavenly places in Christ Jesus: That in the ages to come he might shew the exceeding riches of his grace in his kindness toward us through Christ Jesus. For by grace ye are saved, through faith; and that not of yourselves: it is the gift of God. Not of works, lest any man should boast. For we are his workmanship, created in Christ Jesus unto to good works, which God hath before ordained that we should walk in them." What a wonderful Savior we have.

Furthermore, in Philippians 4:6–8, Paul reminds us to "Be careful for nothing; but in everything by prayer and supplication with thanksgiving let your request be made known unto God. And the peace of God, which passeth all understanding, shall keep your hearts and minds through Christ Jesus. Finally, brethren whatsoever things are true, whatsoever things are honest, whatsoever things are just, whatsoever things are pure, whatsoever things are pure, whatsoever things are of good report; if there be any virtue, and if there be any praise, think on these things."

Grieving is a natural part of humans, as it is a natural part of God, for God grieved for the world in its lost state. He also grieved when He sent His beloved Son and Savior of the world—our Savior and Master Jesus Christ—to hang on that cruel cross as the sacrifice for our sin (*sin*, in this analogy, is plural, for man has many and they are varied). "Those things which ye have both learned, and received and heard, and seen in me, do: and the God of peace shall be with you" (Phil. 4:9). Paul had many struggles and many losses during his journey to that final city prepared for those that love and obey God. But he never turned back, and he never lost hope. Even when hope eluded him, he stayed the course.

The only way to get through the loss of a precious, precious loved one is to go through the stages of grief and to allow yourself to feel everything. It is a cleansing process. It is equal to clearing a road of debris in order to resume your journey.

This is what happened to Sage. She had to clear the road of debris so she could resume her journey through life by faith on the way to that city whose builder and maker is God. "For he looked for a city which has foundations, whose builder and maker is God" (Heb. 11:10). She had once again found a firmer foundation upon which to build her faith.

God does not send evil into the world. Evil lives in the world every day with us. Evil is hanging around. Evil, pain, and disease is of its author, Satan. He is a most formidable opponent (adversary) on the Earth.

He is the ruler of Earth, not of the world. God has set boundaries for him, as he has the rest of his creation: "And hath made of one blood all nations of men and hath determined the times before appointed, and the boundaries of their habitation" (Acts 17:26). Satan has pre-appointed days and times, as man does. His days are numbered, just as man's are.

Satan puts a great amount of effort into gathering souls with which to spend eternity. He lost his soul when he swept up to heaven to war with God; he lost, naturally. Prince Michael and his angels were more than he bargained for. Christ said in Luke 10:18, "I beheld Satan like lightning fall from Heaven." This is how quickly God threw him out—lightning is nanoseconds fast. Nano is instantaneous, quick, split-second, or any other adjective that can describe extremely fast.

Therefore, he does what he can to destroy God's people. Sickness, disease, war, tumult, unhappiness, stress, and any other act that will cause man pain and suffering, he makes happen. In doing so, he fulfills his hope of separating man from God, one person at a time. "Remember,"

Sage said, "Satan has hope too—hope that man will leave serving God and serve him." Satan wants man to battle with temptation. The type of temptation that Satan provides is dependent upon what or where humans' weaknesses lay. Clouded judgment is a lure of Satan. He is the author of confusion and not peace. Whether mental or emotional peace, he is having none of it.

He knows he can't destroy our souls, so he destroys what he can—our personal bodies and anything in this physical world. Satan, like the wind, cannot be seen. But we can see the results of the wind, just as we can see the results of an encounter with Satan. Doing battle with Satan requires the aid of God. Man is no match for Satan; you are a loser from the beginning. He is your adversary. The definition of *adversary* is an opponent, antagonist, enemy, foe, rival, or competitor. Satan is all of these synonyms; he lays a constant barrage on the line he has drawn between man and God, daring that we would have the courage to cross while under fire. God is his enemy, and we are soldiers in His army. Therefore, Satan wages a constant war with His people.

Sage said she sees Satan as an air man: "He is truly an air man; he is always hanging around." Furthermore, Sage said she likens Satan to a tornado. He destroys and sucks up everything in his path and leaves a wake of destruction, misery, pain, and heartache. But on the other hand, he is the speaker of sweet, alluring words that draw you in. Beware of this lure. It is akin to the saying that Sage's mother quoted to her children all their growing years: "Come into my web said the spider to the fly." Satan's lure is a trap. This hurricane has a tail also. Remember the destruction. Those who live on the Gulf Coast know the effects of the hurricane, the eye of the storm, as well as the tail. The eye of a hurricane is just the beginning. Watch for the tail. Don't let the temporary calm fool you.

The best Satan can do is distract humans and take our focus from God; that is why the Scripture admonishes us to walk circumspectfully, redeeming the time because the days are evil: "Wherefore, He saith, Awake thou that sleepth, and arise from the dead, and Christ shall give thee light. See that ye walk circumspectfully, not as fools, but as wise, redeeming the time because the days are evil" (Eph. 5:14–18).

Sage said, "In addition, Satan is like a roaring lion. The temperament of a lion is finding a prey, stalking it (to see its habits or watch for a convenient opportunity), and waiting to pounce and destroy. You do not stand a chance with a lion. He is big, ferocious, and overpowering—the perfect description of Satan, our adversary. You do not stand a chance with Satan without Christ."

Job 1:6–12 gives a perfect description of the wiles and power of Satan. He bids for our souls; he destroys also. Because he can gain man's attention by using the methods of hurt and pain he causes, naturally he knows that through the weakness of the flesh we cannot concentrate on God. He definitely knows how to get our attention.

> *Job 1:6–12: And there was a day when the sons of God cane to present themselves before the Lord, and Satan came also among them. And the Lord said unto Satan, whence comest thou? Then Satan answered the Lord, and said, from going to and fro in the earth, and from walking up and down on it. And the Lord said unto Satan, hast thou considered my servant Job, that there is none like him in the earth, a perfect and an upright man, one that feareth God, and escheweth evil? Then Satan answered the Lord, and said, doth Job fear God for nought? Hast not thou made a hedge about him, and about his house, and about all that he hath on every side? Thou hast blessed the work of his hands, and his substance is increased in the land. But put forth thine hand now, and touch all that he hath, and he will curse thee to thy face. And the Lord said unto Satan, behold, all that he hath is in thy power; only upon himself, put not forth thine hand, so Satan went forth from the presence of the Lord.*

Satan's journey is down the wide way. God's journey is the narrow way. Sage said she went down the wide way for a period of time before she came to where the two ways diverged. She realized that even the wide way leads us to God, as does the narrow way. Both wide ways and narrow way lead to God and eternal life—the narrow way to heaven and an eternity of unspeakable joy and partaking of the tree of life set in the mist of heaven. The wide way leads to an eternity of damnation with Satan, who can only offer pain and suffering (Matt. 7:13–14). God is the maker of all, including Satan. Therefore everyone answers to God at their journey's end.

Sage saw finally what Helen Keller meant when she said, "If the blind put their hand in God's they find their way more surely than those who see but have not faith or purpose" (The Bible Readers Journal, 2001).

Sage was most surely in this state. She saw but had no faith and could see no purpose in the Almighty Creator of the world. Before her life would be rich again, Sage knew she must become blind to the lures of the world in order to see clearly and have faith and purpose once again.

Man on a whole must become blind in order to see. Humans cannot see and have faith or purpose according to their sight. They must trust in God and become blind to their faith and purpose, for it does not mirror God's; His way is the narrow way, and man must become blind to the world in order to have sight for God.

Sage likened herself to a silhouette. A silhouette is like a shadow, an illusion that has no permanency to it. A silhouette has no depth; it can be changed or altered. This is what Sage suffered as a silhouette; she changed from light to dark and then back to light, which has permanency. That light was God, our Lord and Savior Jesus Christ. Unless we are true to the Word of God and true in our resolve to serve God, we can only be silhouettes.

All men have a silhouette. Where are you living? Are you living in darkness or the light? Sage had to answer this question and look at reality like it was. She had to shift the blame from God. She felt as if she was living someone else's life, not her own. Where had she been these last years? Where had her journey taken her?

We all have a second-self to ourselves. Do we know this person that lives within us? Whether this person is spiritual or carnal?

> *Matthew 7:13–14: Enter ye into the strait gate: for wide is the gate, and broad is the way, that leadeth to destruction, and many there be which go in there at. Because strait is the gate, and narrow is the way, which leadeth into life, and few there be that find it.*

What is this person capable of, or who we can become when we are faced with pressures of life or unbearable pain from the loss of a loved one?

Sage said she had to look around to see if there was someone behind her who had thought and done these things. There are no practice sessions with God. We live and serve each day as He promised in the Bible. We are only promised one day at a time. We must try to get as much "right" as humanly possible.

We are flesh and subject to error, but we do not and cannot serve God with flesh. We can only serve Him with our hearts through the spirit or with the Spirit of Christ (Rom. 8:5–10). God did not promise us a shadow of salvation, but He gave His only begotten Son that whosoever believeth in Him and is baptized shall be saved. This promise stands true under the shadow of God's wings. His children can see eternity and live in eternity. This earthly kingdom is but a shadow of what is to come (Heb. 10:1).

Being apathetic or lethargic is spiritually deadly. Sage finally had a relationship, a true relationship, an intimacy, and a bond worshipping God in spirit and in truth. The Father seeketh those who will worship him. God is a spirit, and they that worship Him must worship Him in spirit and in truth (John 4:23–24).

Sage was now singing a new song, ascribing to Him glory and honor, (Rev. 5:9a). Blessing are to the man whom God will not impute sin (Rom. 4:8).

> *Hebrews 10:1: For the law having a shadow of good things to come, and not the very image of the things, can never with those sacrifices which they offered year-by-year continually make the comer thereunto perfect.*
>
> *Romans 4:8: Blessed is the man to whom the Lord will not impute sin.*
>
> *Romans 8:5–10: For they that are after the flesh do mind the things of the flesh; but they that are after the spirit the things of the Spirit. For to be carnally minded*

> *is death; but to be spiritual minded is life and peace. Because the carnal mind is enmity against God; for it is not subject to the law of God, neither indeed can be. So then they that are in the flesh cannot please God. Nut ye are not in the flesh, but in the spirit, if so be that the Spirit of God dwell in you. Now, if any men have not the Spirit of Christ, he is none of his. And if Christ be in you, the body is dead because of sin; but the Spirit is life because of righteousness.*

How much are you willing to pay for the experience of leaving God and following the way of the world because you suffered tragedy in your life?

How will your anger toward God benefit you?

Johann Wolfgang van Goethe wrote a two-part tragedy of Faust's deal with the devil. Faust made a deal (or pact) with the devil in his quest for the true essence of life; he had all he asked for, but all too soon, death followed …

Sage, like Eve, suffered a spiritual death and became estranged from God, which is a sin. Sin is described as actions by which humans rebel against God, miss His purpose for their lives, surrender the power of evil rather than to God, and become estranged from God. Sin is an attitude of rebellion against God. Rebellion was at the root of the problem from Adam and Eve (Gen. 3) and has been at the root of humanity's plight ever since. The Bible has a rich vocabulary for sin: too miss the mark, crooked or perverse spirit, and violence.

Sin is the lack of fellowship with God. Anything that disturbs or distorts this fellowship is a sin. The New Testament defines sin against the backdrop of Jesus's perfection as the standard for righteousness. Sin has terrible by-products. One terrible by-product of sin is death. Continual, consistent sin will bring spiritual death to a person who has not come under the lordship of Christ through repentance and faith (Rom. 6:23; Rev. 20:14).

Christ has negated the power of Satan in making death horrible and has freed the person from slavery to this awful fear (Heb. 2:14–15). Sin brings separation from, estrangement from, and a lack of fellowship with God. If a person dies not having corrected this problem by trusting Christ, then the separation becomes permanent (Rom. 6:23). Sin also produces estrangement from other people. All interpersonal problems have sin as their root cause (James 4:1–3). The only hope to achieve peace on either the personal or national level is through Jesus Christ, the Prince of Peace (Master Study Bible's Cornerstone Encyclopedia of Bible Knowledge 2001, B-462–B-463).

God doesn't make deals; He commands, and we follow. That is why He is God and Satan is Satan. The only thing Satan can offer man is a deal—a bad deal.

The temptation and tragedy of Faust can be compared to the temptation and tragedy of the story of Job in the Scripture. Job resisted his temptation and passed his test, all of them, no matter the difficultyJob, chapters 1 and 2. But Faust?

Sage paid a high price for her choice, but thanks be to God, she found her way once again.

The bonds of the world have been broken; the anger is gone; the blaming has stopped; the pain is still there, but it is manageable. Scars heal, but how you got the scar will forever be there. You do not forget the trails and tribulations you have gone through, but you learn to live in an "acceptance" mode.

Nothing in the world is worth the loss of one's soul. The psalmist reminds us in Psalms 49:7 that none of them can redeem his brother by any means, not even by giving to God a ransom for him. Each of us have a cross to bear for Christ. He did not say what that cross would be. It could be death, sickness, tragedy, or any other of that that besets humans. "And he that taketh not his cross and followeth after me is not worthy of me. For Christ sayeth: He that findeth his life shall lose it; and he that loseth his life for my sake shall find it" (Matt. 10:38–39).

Sage had lost her life and found it again.

> *Roman 6:23: For the wages of sin is death; but the gift of God is eternal life through Jesus Christ our Lord.*

> *Revelations 20:14: And death and hell were cast into the lake of fire. This is the second death.*

Hebrews 2:14–15: Forasmuch then as the children are partakers of flesh and blood, he also himself likewise took part of the same, that through death he might destroy him that had the power of death, that is, the devil.

References

http://definitions.dictionary.com/adversary

Anonymous. Grieve Not for Me. http://www.funeralprogram.site.com

Cornerstone Encyclopedia of Bible Knowledge: Master Bible. 2001. Nashville: Cornerstone Bible Publishers.

Dunbar, Pal L. We Wear the Mask. www.poemhunter.com/poetry.dunbar/section7/rhtml.

January 9, 2010.

Elwell, Walter A. 2008. *Baker Commentary on the Bible*, 5th ed. Based on the NIV. Grand Rapids: Baker Books.

Frost, Robert. "The Road Not Taken." www.poemhunter.com/poetry/frost/section7.rhtml. January 9, 2010.

Gay, Robert. 1994. "On Bended Knees I Come." *Songs of Faith and Praise. Integrity's Hosanna Music.* West Monroe: Howard Publishing Company.

Goethe, Johann von Wolfgang: Faust: (1749-1832). En.gethe-faust.org.

International Bible Society. 1984. *Holy Bible, New International Version (NIV)*. Grand Rapids: Zondervan Press.

http://definitions.dictionary.net//darkness

Johnson, Julia H. 1994. "Grace Greater Than All Our Sins." *Songs of Faith and Praise*. West Monroe: Howard Publishing Company.

Keller, Helen. 2001. "If the blind put their hand in God's they find their way more surely than those who see but have not faith or purpose." *The Bible Reader's Journal*. Fort Worth: The Brown Low Corporation.

The King James Master Study Bible. 2001. Nashville: Cornerstone Bible Publishers.

Lao-Tu. The Journey of A Thousand Miles begins with One Step. http://quotationspage.com. December 3, 2011.

Littlejohn, S. and K. Foss. 2008. *Theories of Human Communication*, 9th ed. Belmont: Thomas & Wadsworth.

Longfellow, Henry Wadsworth: The Psalm of Life. www.poemhunter.com

MacMillan, Richard, Free Spread the Wings of Mystery; www.richard.mcmillan.com.

Rock of Gibraltar, The. http://gibraltar.coastsur.com.

Roosevelt, Theodore: A thorough knowledge of the Bible is worth more than a college education: *The Bible Reader's Journal, 2001*. Brownlow Corporation, Fort Worth, Texas.

Songs of Faith and Praise. 1994. "Song It is well with my soul." West Monroe: Howard Publishing Company.

Stevenson, Mary. 1984. "Footprints in the Sand" Footprints-in the-sand.com. www.footprints-inthe-sand.com/PoemPage.htm.

Tozer, A.W. God did not write a book and send it by messenger to: *The Bible Reader's Journal, 2001*. Brownlow Corporation, Fort Worth, Texas.

About the Author

Carlotta Maria Shinn-Russell is a resident of Mobile, Alabama. She is a wife, mother, and a career-oriented individual. She loves to read, teach, write, and listen to music, including classical, symphony, rock and roll, and country.

Some of her favorite things include *To Kill a Mockingbird*, John Wayne, David Letterman, *Face the Nation*, farming, lazy Sunday afternoons in the country, grilled salmon at Olive Garden, baked catfish, tuna, green tea, decaf Maxwell House Coffee (she likes to grind her own coffee as well), art, decorating, fashions, shoes, and accessories.

Carlotta holds a BBA, MBA, and MA in communications. She currently works as executive assistant to the president of Alabama School of Mathematics and Science (asms.net) and is also a speech instructor at Jefferson Davis Community College and is a professor of small business management, business communication, and economics at Faulkner University, Mobile branch.

She is professionally involved with the American Association of University Women, Professional Writers Association of America, American Folklore Society of America, and the Stanford Who's Who of Accomplished Professional in Business and Education for 2011–2012.

She and her family are active members of the Azalea City Church of Christ.

About the Book

The book *Changes: From Spiritual Hopelessness To Spiritual Hope* carries readers on a journey of pain, heartache, loss of a loved one, loss of spirituality, anger, blame, an encounter with the world, and the journey back to God after the discovery.

www.ingramcontent.com/pod-product-compliance
Lightning Source LLC
Chambersburg PA
CBHW060403080526
44583CB00012B/453